Centaur Art

Remo Pareschi

Centaur Art

The Future of Art in the Age of Generative AI

Springer

Remo Pareschi
Stake Lab
University of Molise
Campobasso, Italy

ISBN 978-3-031-69062-4 ISBN 978-3-031-69063-1 (eBook)
https://doi.org/10.1007/978-3-031-69063-1

Cover illustration: The image on the cover was created by the author in DALL-E, using prompts such as "stylized," "abstract," "centaur" and "modern artistic style." The visually striking representation embodies the fusion of human and machine, capturing the essence of centauric intelligence explored throughout the book.

This Springer imprint is published by the registered company Springer Nature Switzerland AG
The registered company address is: Gewerbestrasse 11, 6330 Cham, Switzerland

Nothing is original. Steal from anywhere that resonates with inspiration or fuels your imagination. Devour old films, new films, music, books, paintings, photographs, poems, dreams, random conversations, architecture, bridges, street signs, trees, clouds, bodies of water, light and shadows. Select only things to steal from that speak directly to your soul. If you do this, your work (and theft) will be authentic. Authenticity is invaluable; originality is nonexistent.

Jim Jarmusch, Cinematographer

The secret to a masterpiece is 10 percent inspiration and 90 percent perspiration.

Mario Vargas Llosa, Writer

To Grazia

Preface

This book ventures into the dynamic interplay between art, human creativity, and artificial ingenuity, marking a significant turning point in knowledge and creativity traditionally perceived as uniquely human. This narrative's heart is the synergy between human and artificial intelligence, a catalyst for innovation and creative exploration in various fields. *Centaur Art* draws inspiration from this synergy for its title and central theme. The centaur, a mythological creature embodying the union between man and horse, serves as a metaphor for the complex and multifaceted collaboration between man and machine. It thus encompasses the fusion of human and artificial creativity and lays the foundation for an in-depth model of their interaction and integration.

The book's onset illustrates how the principles of centauric collaboration transcend the boundaries of art, with fields as diverse as design, planning, healthcare, military strategy, finance, customer relationship management, and software development testifying to the rise and expansion of centauric systems. While anchoring a significant part of the discussion within the art world, the book broadens its horizon to imagine a future in which such hybrid systems significantly expand and redefine diverse sectors.

Why, then, start with a focus on art? The motivation lies in the intricate blend of controversy, cognition, and the socioeconomic ramifications accompanying the rise of artificial intelligence within this domain. Like technological advancements of the past—photography, cinema, the Internet, Web, social media, and content creation tools like Photoshop—AI is reshaping the foundational principles of artistic engagement and production. This dynamic evolution, replete with complexities and potential pitfalls, has spurred my interest and inquiry.

The book opens by revisiting the arguments of Walter Benjamin, a pivotal figure in German philosophy and sociology whose legacy was tragically cut short by the Nazi regime. In his essay *The Work of Art in the Age of Its Technical Reproducibility*, Benjamin regarded the advent of mass media like cinema with apprehension and awe. These innovations, he predicted, would dramatically transform the dissemination of visual content, establishing an industry capable of reaching vast audiences beyond the constraints of physical location. This proliferation of accessible communication will intensify with the emergence of the Internet, Web, and social media, marking a significant departure from the exclusivity of early twentieth-century avant-garde movements such as Surrealism, Expressionism, Cubism, and Futurism. While these artistic revolutions challenged and redefined conventional art, they inadvertently cemented its status as a pursuit for the elite. On the other hand, the introduction of mass and social media heralded a new era in producing visual content—one that embraces broader participation and consumption, evident in the popularity of comics, fan art, and video game characters. Imagine, if you will, an avant-garde luminary from the first half of the twentieth century—be it André Breton, Pablo Picasso, Marcel Duchamp, or Salvador Dalí (whose legacy extends to the ensuing discussion through the AI tool named DALL-E)—encountering a generative AI platform. How might they have reacted? Their fascination would likely be profound, as such technology would offer unparalleled means to actualize many avant-garde theories. These include challenging the fidelity of art to reality—a hallmark of classical art; using painting as a conduit to the unconscious; exploring the nexus between writing and painting; and redefining the notions of authorship and artwork.

In stark contrast, content creators a century later have often greeted these tools with skepticism, if not outright hostility, viewing them primarily as content thieves and usurpers of roles traditionally ascribed to humans. Yet, this technological progression—including photography, cinema, television, the Web, the Internet, and editing tools like Photoshop—has facilitated the widespread dissemination of human creativity. The emergence of generative AI, the next evolutionary leap, is now met with significant concern and is perceived as a looming threat. This stark resistance underscores a shift toward a more defensive and apprehensive stance regarding integrating technology in creative processes, highlighting a deepening rift between technological potential and public acceptance.

This dichotomy underpins one of this book's core motivations: Can we harmonize human creativity with technological advancement, leading us into an era of hybrid intelligence and creativity? The "centauric model" offers a framework for this reconciliation. Aimed at integrating human and artificial creativity, it represents one possible approach and a pressing area for thorough exploration and understanding in our time.

Embarking on the mission to define the centauric model rigorously required moving beyond its initial intuitive understanding. Therefore, I adopted a bottom-up construction strategy, beginning with an analysis that juxtaposed two centauric instances: the well-known yet fundamentally flawed centauric chess and the promising domain of centauric art. This comparison illuminated the prerequisites for successful centaurization within creative practices, outlining a conceptual framework for identifying where functional systems could thrive.

This comparative approach proved doubly enlightening. Examining the AI technologies powering chess engines and generative art platforms uncovered significant overlaps, suggesting the efficacy of centauric systems hinges not solely on technological capabilities but on the cognitive and socioeconomic milieu from which they emerge. The leverage of robust methodologies and theories from systems theory and cognitive architectures was instrumental in understanding and delineating this broader context. These disciplines provided the necessary scaffolding to rigorously articulate the conditions under which centauric collaborations could flourish, underscoring that the success of these hybrid models depends as much on their technological underpinnings as on the cultural and intellectual ecosystems they inhabit.

While bringing the centauric model to life involved laying its conceptual and theoretical foundations, exploring its tangible application in artistic creation was also paramount. The latter effort was twofold: direct experimentation unveiled its innovative potential—most notably, the capacity to merge symbolic content production methods with traditional, analog techniques like painting. Simultaneously, endeavors were showcased by artists who have seamlessly integrated this hybrid practice into their work. To clarify these processes, I employed flowcharts and diagrams, rendering artistic production as a tangible domain akin yet distinct to seemingly less "creative" fields such as engineering and design. This methodological choice emphasizes that despite its unique characteristics, artistic practice hinges on structured and collaborative efforts that are not dissimilar to those found in other disciplines. Indeed, a significant portion of current public discourse harbors apprehensions about diminishing human artistic creativity in the face of AI advancements. Such concerns largely stem from a mythologized view of the artist's role. History, however, tells us that artists—across eras and irrespective of the acknowledged artistic value of their works—have consistently engaged in complex, organized processes, often relying on extensive networks of collaborators.

In conclusion, this work can also stimulate reflections on the broader topic of the future and the foundations of artificial intelligence. Despite significant strides in the field, the quest for Artificial General Intelligence (AGI)—an intelligence endowed with human-like adaptability—remains a distant goal, possibly as the consequence of a conceptual misalignment: while true generality in intelligence, be it natural or artificial, arises from its systemic and holistic properties, current approaches often view it through a reductionist lens. This perspective not only narrows the scope of intelligence but also introduces conceptual inconsistencies.

For humanity, general intelligence evolved through the intricate interplay between Homo Sapiens and their environment. The fusion of natural and artificial intelligence in centauric systems paves the way toward a new, holistically conceived form of general intelligence that may be less elusive than one defined through traditional reductionist frameworks.

Milan, Italy
May 2024

Remo Pareschi

Acknowledgments

This book owes its existence to the contributions and encouragement of many, some of whom may not fully realize the extent of their influence. Among these, Hervé Gallaire was particularly supportive. As a former colleague and supervisor in two prior endeavors, I was fortunate to reconnect with him after a significant hiatus. Our discussions increasingly focused on this project, with Hervé offering crucial insights that shaped its development. He is a thorough and thoughtful reader whose feedback was essential in refining the manuscript, helping to clarify ambiguities and correct inaccuracies. His interest in generative artificial intelligence, especially in its application to visual content, made him a valuable source of information on the subject's broader implications.

Hervé also made sure to keep me updated with relevant news and articles, ensuring that I remained well-informed about the latest developments in this rapidly evolving field. His contributions have been greatly appreciated, helping me to navigate a complex landscape filled with innovation.

My gratitude extends to Nicola Noviello, with whom my exploration into the creative use of generative artificial intelligence began, particularly its integration into computational architectures for artistic production. My journey continued with Enrico Aldorasi and Francesco Salzano, building upon the groundwork laid with Nicola.

I am also grateful to Alexandru Ciolan from Springer for his support and help throughout the project. His assistance was instrumental in guiding the book to publication, and his expertise in handling the editorial aspects was most valuable.

None of this would have been feasible without an environment conducive to productivity and intellectual creativity. In my experience, such creativity flourishes only within a context of tranquility and positive emotions. This nurturing atmosphere was generously provided by Grazia, to whom this book is lovingly dedicated.

Contents

The Rise of Centauric Systems

In 1935, at the height of the Nazi regime in Germany, Walter Benjamin wrote an essay entitled *The Work of Art in the Age of its Technical Reproducibility* [1], in which he noted how artistic production had changed radically due to the emergence of new technologies, such as cameras and film cameras. These technologies allowed the mass reproduction of works of art, similar to the mass production techniques that had transformed the way factories worked. Benjamin was a philosopher, cultural critic, and writer of the Frankfurt School, a group of intellectuals who applied an unorthodox Marxist perspective to analyze culture and society. His main interests were aesthetics, culture, and technology.

Benjamin's essay remains relevant in light of recent developments in art generated through artificial intelligence (AI). The technologies he writes about were instrumental in the rise of the film industry but were also exploited for political propaganda by totalitarian regimes such as Fascist Italy and Nazi Germany. Benjamin reflected on how, by allowing the systematic reproduction of works of art, these could degrade their "aura," a term by which he meant the unique and authentic presence of a work linked to its historical and cultural context. He also pointed out how these technologies could "aestheticize" political ideas, making them seem more attractive and acceptable using artistic forms and techniques. But he also appreciated its positive potential to democratize art and make it more accessible to the public.

Almost 90 years later, we are entering the era of the technical constructability of art, the source of a new upheaval in artistic production. Today's technology goes beyond reproducibility, leveraging artificial intelligence to generate digital artworks that adapt to pre-photographic and pre-cinematic practices, such as painting, writing, and music. Such "generative AI" has the ability, starting from learned rules and models, to create new content ranging from images (the focus of this book) to text (through AI assistants such as the popular ChatGPT) to further types of content, such as music and videos. Although Benjamin's arguments are still valid, raising questions that are worth re-proposing and trying to answer in the current context, an even broader question looms, crossing the scientific and artistic community and

R. Pareschi, *Centaur Art*, https://doi.org/10.1007/978-3-031-69063-1_1

world public opinion: Will the advent of generative AI spell the end of human dominance in art, if not in all creative activities?

Indeed, the implications of generative AI on human creativity are the subject of intense debate among experts, business leaders, professional and artistic communities, and the general public. To give indicative samples of the ongoing discussion, articles like Harvard Business Review's *How Generative AI Could Disrupt Creative Work*[1] and Forbes' *Human Borgs: How Artificial Intelligence Can Kill Creativity And Make Us Dumb*[2] offer foreboding views on the future of human creativity in the age of artificial intelligence; on the other hand, the study *Navigating the Jagged Technological Frontier: Field Experimental Evidence of the Effects of AI on Knowledge Worker Productivity and Quality*, conducted by Harvard Business School on the Boston Consulting Group [2], shows that artificial intelligence can augment human capabilities rather than replace them. The study found that those consultants who used ChatGPT were more productive and produced higher-quality results. Adobe Chief Product Officer Scott Belsky held similarly optimistic views at an event hosted by Cornell Tech focused on AI-powered visual content production.[3] This perspective tunes well with the one we will pursue in this book.

Origin and Evolution of the Centauric Model

Artificial intelligence (AI) has long ventured beyond the confines of research facilities, captivating both the media and the public's imagination. Originating in the 1940s and 1950s as a groundbreaking field, AI has since diversified, seamlessly blending scientific breakthroughs with transformative technological applications to redefine our societal and economic terrains.

Initially, AI's ambitious objective was to replicate human intelligence by pursuing artificial general intelligence (AGI) to mirror the full spectrum of human cognition through computational methods. This enduring aspiration has not been without its controversies, especially concerning the potential dystopian ramifications of AGI. Fears of malevolent super-intelligences intent on dominating or even eradicating humanity have been voiced.

However, for many years, AI's most notable successes happened in 'narrow AI,' mimicking and often outperforming specific human abilities in areas like strategic gaming and quiz competitions. Yet, recent advancements suggest we might be close to AGI by emulating broader human capabilities. Central to this book is exploring one such capability: artistic creativity. We will delve into this subject from the perspective of a partnership between human and machine intelligence. Indeed,

---

[1] Source: https://hbr.org/2023/04/how-generative-ai-could-disrupt-creative-work.

[2] Source: https://www.forbes.com/sites/nelsongranados/2022/01/31/human-borgs-how-artificial-intelligence-can-kill-creativity-and-make-us-dumber/?sh=37ebd93f21a2.

[3] Source: https://tech.cornell.edu/news/ai-vs-artist-the-future-of-creativity/.

contrary to the bleak narrative of machines overshadowing human creativity, we posit that this union is the harbinger of a fruitful era of collaborative enhancement.

Centaur Chess: An Instructive Failure

Artificial intelligence is currently grappling with artistic creativity by generating artworks of various genres and of ever-higher technical quality. This situation naturally raises questions about the future of human art, echoing and amplifying the uproar that lashed out in 1997 when IBM's Deep Blue program defeated Garry Kasparov, one of the greatest chess masters ever. Since then, AI has continued to widen the gap with humans in chess and other complex games like Shogi and Go.

This event, which demonstrated AI's superiority over humans in a strategic game, gave rise to the concept of 'centaur' in AI. The term originates from Greek mythology and refers to a chimera creature combining a human's upper body with a horse's lower body. These mythical beings embodied both the rationality and emotions of humans and the raw strength and speed of horses. Drawing from this mythological imagery, the term in the context of artificial intelligence symbolizes the fusion of two distinct entities, each bringing its unique strengths to the table.

The centaur approach in AI embodies a collaborative model where humans and machines work together. Machines can process vast amounts of data and perform complex calculations faster and more accurately than humans. Simultaneously, humans offer insights, creativity, and emotional intelligence that machines cannot match. This synergy, often referred to as augmented or hybrid intelligence, has the potential to surpass the capabilities of either entity working in isolation.

In chess, a domain where the centauric model has been applied early and extensively, machines use brute-force searching, a systematic approach that maximizes computational power through sophisticated heuristics and optimizations. These engines can evaluate millions of potential moves within seconds, pinpointing the optimal one for any chess position. Thus, their computational prowess is undeniable, yet they lack the nuanced understanding, intuition, and creativity that human players bring to the game. Centaur chess, or advanced or cyborg chess,[4] is a format where human players collaborate with chess machines to merge the human's intuitive and creative capabilities with the machine's analytical might. Kasparov was one of the main proponents of this approach, suggesting that it could challenge the prevailing notion of AI's dominance in the game. The underlying belief was that while machines can calculate moves with unparalleled speed and accuracy, humans can provide strategic insights, recognize patterns, and introduce innovative strategies that machines might overlook.

However, the rapid advancement of technology, especially since the early 2010s, has disrupted this balance. Chess machines have become more powerful and

[4] Source: https://en.wikipedia.org/wiki/Advanced_chess.

efficient, overshadowing the human input in centaur chess. The gap in ELO ratings[5] between human and artificial players illustrates this trend. As of their match date in 1997, Kasparov and Deep Blue had ELO ratings of around 2800. Today, Deep Blue's strongest descendant, Stockfish, has an ELO rating of over 3600, while the strongest human player, Magnus Carlsen, has an ELO of 2900. This growing gap between the strength of human and artificial players went hand in hand with the diminishing human contribution to centaur chess. Indeed, while it may seem that a team combining a 3600 ELO machine with a 2900 ELO human should be stronger than a single 3600 ELO machine, this is not the case. The human's slower analysis and potential for error can actually hinder the team's performance. Additionally, the machine's computational abilities often already encompass the human's strategic insights, making the human contribution redundant. The team's ELO, therefore, tends to reflect that of the stronger player, not the sum of both. This underscores the diminishing role of the human in centaur chess as technology advances.

Moreover, a pivotal development occurred in 2017 when AlphaZero, an AI developed by the Google company DeepMind, defeated Stockfish in a 100-game match. Unlike its predecessors, AlphaZero employs machine-learning techniques to simulate human-like intuition and strategic depth—traits traditionally viewed as exclusive to human players. This advancement in AI capabilities starkly challenges the notion that human intuition and creativity provide a competitive edge in centaur chess. AlphaZero's performance not only matches but may surpass the strategic insights of the world's best human players, delivering a decisive blow to any lingering claims of a significant human role in competing against or collaborating with chess engines.

Thus, as artificial players progress and their capabilities expand, the competition for chess supremacy has become a private affair between purely artificial players. Engines like AlphaZero and its open-source clone, Leela, have shown increasing intuition and creativity. Meanwhile, brute-force engines like Stockfish have upgraded their technology to compete on par with machine learning-based artificial players. For humans, whether autonomous or part of centaur structures, it seems that strategy games have now reached a "game over" scenario.

Reclaiming the Centauric Model: Success Across Disciplines

Despite these setbacks in domains like chess, the centauric model has persisted and experienced a resurgence. Recent advancements in artificial intelligence, machine

[5] The ELO rating system is a method for calculating the relative skill levels of players in zero-sum games such as chess. It is named after its creator Arpad Elo, a Hungarian-American physics professor and chess master. It works by assigning a numerical rating to each player based on their previous results in rated games. The rating reflects the probability of a player winning or losing against other players with different ratings. The higher the rating, the stronger the player.

learning, and the pervasive digital transformation across various sectors drive this renewed interest. The model has been found relevant in diverse fields such as government, education, healthcare, finance, law, corporate governance, conversational AI, and the military. While it may have limitations in narrowly defined areas like chess and other strategy games, the centaur approach is particularly effective in fields that demand a holistic understanding and integration within a broader context. For instance, in government, it assists policymakers in harmonizing data-driven insights with human values; in education, it enhances learning through personalized feedback and mentorship; and in healthcare, it improves diagnostic and therapeutic accuracy by merging medical expertise with machine learning.

This revival and broad applicability of the centauric model not only mirror contemporary technological advancements but also realize the foresight of information technology pioneers from the 1960s. These visionaries had anticipated and conceptualized the integration of humans and machines. Douglas Engelbart, renowned for inventing the computer mouse and his groundbreaking work in interactive computing, showcased a 1968 demonstration famously known as *The Mother of All Demos*. This presentation featured real-time text editing, video conferencing, and hypertext, laying the groundwork for the future of personal computing and the Internet. In his 1962 article *Augmenting Human Intellect: A Conceptual Framework* [3], Engelbart defined augmentation as "increasing a person's capability to approach complex problem situations, gain comprehension to meet specific needs, and derive solutions to problems." He applied this concept to the human-computer relationship, arguing that humans, limited in their capacity to process and manipulate information, could overcome these constraints by using computers to augment their cognitive abilities. Engelbart proposed that computers should be capable of displaying and manipulating various types of information, such as text, graphics, audio, and video, and provide interactive feedback and guidance to users. He also envisioned a collaborative work system where humans and computers could work together in teams, coordinating their activities through a network of computers.

Preceding Engelbart, J.C.R. Licklider, a psychologist and computer scientist who foresaw the Web three decades before its existence, published *Man-Computer Symbiosis* in 1960 [4]. In this paper, Licklider defined symbiosis as "the mutually beneficial coexistence of two dissimilar organisms" and applied this concept to the human-computer relationship. He posited that combining the distinct strengths and compensating for the weaknesses of humans and computers could achieve higher performance and intelligence than either. Licklider envisioned computers that could communicate with humans in natural language, process information rapidly and accurately, store and retrieve vast amounts of data, and adapt to the needs and preferences of users. He also anticipated a network of interconnected computers, enabling global access and information sharing.

Thus, let's leap about 60 years in the future and, from the contributions ahead of the time of Engelbart and Licklider, let's rejoin the present day, crossing the intermediate and semi-aborted stage of centauric chess, to find the centauric models in good health and applied to full swing in a variety of fields and sectors.

Centauric Government

To start with, the introductory chapter of the book *Executive Policymaking: The Role of the OMB in the Presidency* [5] explores the Office of Management and Budget (OMB) through the lens of the centauric model. It highlights the OMB's crucial role in assisting the U.S. President with budgeting, liaising with Congress, and regulatory matters. The chapter emphasizes that the various data analysis and report generation software tools used for this aim are essential but insufficient for the effective operation of the OMB. The expertise of OMB staff is vital for interpreting data, engaging with stakeholders, and advising the President. As a result, the final report is a blend of machine-generated data and human insight. The chapter also delves into the challenges and complexities of implementing the centaur model within the OMB and its interactions with other executive agencies and Congress. It outlines the need for trust-building, transparency, evidence-based decision-making, and flexibility for effective centauric policymaking.

Centauric Military Systems

Similarly, the book *Strategy Strikes Back: How the Star Wars Explains Modern Military Conflict* [6] delves into the complexities of war through the lens of the popular sci-fi saga. It explores how the centauric model can foster better cooperation between soldiers and machines, resulting in more victories and fewer casualties. In fact, the U.S. Air Force is already experimenting with this approach, as The New York Times reported in an article that describes how a human pilot and an AI system teamed up to defeat another AI adversary in a simulated dogfight.[6] The human-AI duo outsmarted and outmaneuvered the enemy AI, demonstrating the potential of combining human intuition and AI speed and accuracy in combat situations.

Centauric Models for the Corporate World

In the tech world, an article from VentureBeat[7] argues that the centauric model is transforming institutional perceptions of artificial intelligence. It highlights its applications across sectors like education, healthcare, finance, and law, emphasizing how human-machine collaboration can solve complex problems more effectively. CIOReview, a magazine focused on enterprise technology, discusses the centaur model's role in resolving the AI-human conflict in the corporate landscape.[8] The

[6] Source: https://www.nytimes.com/2023/08/27/us/politics/ai-air-force.html.

[7] Source: https://venturebeat.com/datadecisionmakers/centaur-rising-how-a-decades-old-paradigm-is-changing-the-way-that-top-institutions-look-at-ai/.

[8] Source: https://artificial-intelligence.cioreview.com/cxoinsight/reconciling-the-aihuman-conflict-with-the-centaur-model-nid-24514-cid-175.html.

article suggests that adopting a centaur approach allows businesses to leverage AI's strengths—such as efficiency, productivity, and innovation—while mitigating weaknesses like bias and ethical concerns. It underscores the synergy between human skills like communication and creativity and machine capabilities like speed and accuracy.

Centauric Healthcare

The special issue of the journal Frontiers in Human Dynamics titled *Human and Artificial Collaboration for Medical Best Practices* [7] explores the potential of human and artificial intelligence collaboration in enhancing healthcare outcomes and quality. This issue features articles concerned with ethical, legal, and social issues and technical challenges. It also showcases case studies and applications across various medical fields, such as telemedicine, orthopedics, cardiology, oncology, and diagnostics. These contributions resonate with the centaur approach, aiming to leverage the unique strengths of both human and artificial agents for a synergistic effect. In a similar vein, the article titled *Algorithm, Human, or the Centaur: How to Enhance Clinical Care?* [8], featured in the Journal of the American Medical Association, zeroes in on healthcare. It scrutinizes the role of machine learning in predicting patient readmissions within 30 days post-organ transplant. The authors develop an algorithm and compare its performance to human experts, finding the algorithm to be more accurate. However, they highlight that trust and proper usage remain challenges. To tackle this, they propose a centauric model where doctors and algorithms collaborate to improve patient outcomes and reduce costs, claiming this approach could lower readmission rates by 26.4%.

The Intrinsic Centaurism of Conversational Agents

Switching gears, Soroush Saghafian, one of the authors of the article [8] cited above and an operations research professor at Harvard, discusses the so far undisputed star of generative AI, ChatGPT, in a blog post.[9] ChatGPT employs natural language processing and machine learning frameworks known as Large Language Models (LLMs) to generate engaging conversations on various topics. Saghafian views ChatGPT as a higher-level application of the centaur concept, emphasizing its autonomous operation while acknowledging its human-designed foundation and training.

Also focusing on ChatGPT and its underlying LLM GPT-4, I introduce an innovative method for assessing the explanatory capabilities of such AI platforms in the article *Abductive Reasoning with the GPT-4 Language Model: Case Studies*

[9] Source: https://scholar.harvard.edu/saghafian/blog/analytics-science-behind-chatgpt-human-algorithm-or-human-algorithm-centaur.

from criminal investigation, medical practice, scientific research [9]. Utilizing a dialogical interview format inspired by Knowledge Elicitation techniques, the study engages human users and the AI model in a collaborative dialogue to formulate plausible hypotheses. The model's efficacy is demonstrated through three diverse case studies—from criminal investigations to medical diagnostics and cosmology. The paper champions an approach where human intelligence and AI work symbiotically, which fits handsomely with the centaur model. In this dynamic, the human user iteratively challenges the AI to refine its hypotheses until a satisfactory conclusion is reached.

This interaction could be further strengthened by applying two techniques that will also be relevant to the theme of artistic creation central to this book, namely *prompt engineering* and *model fine-tuning*. Prompt engineering focuses on shaping the input instructions for the LLMs, such as providing keywords, examples, or templates, helping design better input instructions that elicit more informative and relevant responses from the AI model.[10] For example, prompt engineering can help specify the type of hypothesis the AI model should generate, such as a causal explanation or a counterfactual scenario. Model fine-tuning is a technique that involves training the LLMs on custom datasets that reflect the specific context and domain of each task.[11] Model fine-tuning can help train the AI model on data relevant to the task at hand, such as crime reports, medical records, or scientific papers. For example, it can help improve the accuracy and reliability of the hypotheses generated by the AI model, as well as its domain knowledge and vocabulary. These techniques can improve the collaboration between human users and AI, as well as facilitate more effective and efficient reasoning processes.

Centauric Finance

Concerning financial applications, in the article *Integrating heuristics and learning in a computational architecture for cognitive trading* [10], I present with my co-author a case for hybrid intelligence in the trading sector. The architecture for cognitive robotic trading provided therein integrates human expertise in strategy selection with machine capabilities in data analytics and automated execution. Termed "cognitive trading," this approach elevates trading bots to an intermediate level of intelligence, in between narrow AI and artificial general intelligence. This modular and flexible architecture allows human traders to adapt the system to align with their chosen strategies. It employs a financial heuristic toolbox that combines proven human heuristics with machine learning and evolutionary algorithms, aiming for a synergistic effect that enhances trading outcomes while contributing to the broader goal of advancing toward AGI.

---

[10] Source: https://developer.nvidia.com/blog/an-introduction-to-large-language-models-prompt-engineering-and-p-tuning/.

[11] Source: https://www.allupost.com/blog/prompt-engineering-vs-fine-tuning/.

Centauric Consulting

We have already mentioned the study from the Harvard Business School that assessed the impact of AI on a broad set of tasks in consulting, performed as a controlled scientific experiment on 7% of the Boston Consulting Group workforce [2]. Consultants using AI finished 12.2% more tasks on average, completed tasks 25.1% more quickly, and delivered 40% higher quality results than those who didn't. Ethan Mollick, one of the authors of the study, in a blog summary and commentary of its results titled *Centaurs and Cyborgs on the Jagged AI frontiers*[12] describes how AI gave a solid boost to the productivity of the consultants involved in the experiment. He also points out that for certain tasks, human problem-solving ability remained key; hence, those who relied on uncritical and mechanical use of AI performed worse than those who used it as a complement rather than a replacement for their capabilities. Thus, according to this view, generative AI is an opportunity to augment human capabilities through collaboration on an equal footing rather than a risk of impairment or decline of human creativity.

What Is This Book About?

This book explores generative AI as a complementary force in art, akin to the anatomy of a centaur. We posit that AI, much like in such a mythological creature, serves as a collaborator in the artistic process, enhancing rather than replacing human creativity. The book's structure unfolds as follows:

- Chapter "Art and Artificial Intelligence between Past, Present and Future" discusses generative technologies' social and cultural impact. We will also identify artistic movements and trends of the past that directly harmonize with the perspectives opened up by generative platforms.
- Chapters "AI for Games and Art" and "The Art of Turning Prompts into Art" delve into the technological underpinnings of generative AI, exploring its operational mechanisms, capabilities, and limitations.
- Chapter "The Art of Turning Prompts into Art" introduces examples of centaur art, a theme further pursued in chapters "Art as an Open System" and "From 'On-life' to 'On-art' and 'Beyond-Life'".
- Chapter "Art as an Open System" delves deeper into the cognitive dynamics of centaur art, elucidating why AI is an innovative component in the artistic process rather than a replacement for human ingenuity.
- Chapter "From 'On-life' to 'On-art' and 'Beyond-Life'" concludes the book by showcasing the practicability of new centauric capabilities offered by generative platforms. It includes instances of artists already harnessing these capabilities in their work.

---

[12] Source: https://www.oneusefulthing.org/p/centaurs-and-cyborgs-on-the-jagged.

Central to our exploration is the concept that all art, across millennia, inherently embodies a centauric principle. This principle is rooted in the interplay of diverse cognitive components, where the advent of AI in art is not a displacement but a transformative integration. Like design and engineering, art is fundamentally about creatively engaging with our environment. This involves capturing observations, representing them, and transforming those representations into various forms of creation. AI platforms designed for visual content generation seamlessly integrate into this process, extending human capabilities and opening new avenues for artistic expression and innovation.

References

1. Walter Benjamin. *The Work of Art in the Age of Its Technological Reproducibility, and Other Writings on Media*. Original version: "Das Kunstwerk im Zeitalter seiner technischen Reproduzierbarkeit" first published in the journal Zeitschrift für Sozialforschung in 1936. Harvard University Press, 2008.
2. Fabrizio Dell'Acqua et al. "Navigating the Jagged Technological Frontier: Field Experimental Evidence of the Effects of AI on Knowledge Worker Productivity and Quality". In: *Harvard Business School Technology Operations Mgt. Unit Working Paper* 24–013 (2023). URL: https://papers.ssrn.com/sol3/papers.cfm?abstract_id$=$4573321.
3. Douglas C Engelbart. *Augmenting human intellect: A conceptual framework*. Tech. rep. Stanford Research Institute, 1962.
4. JCR Licklider. "Man-computer symbiosis". In: *IRE Transactions on human factors in electronics* 1 (1960), pp. 4–11.
5. Meena Bose and Andrew Rudalevige, eds. *Executive Policymaking: The Role of the OMB in the Presidency*. Brookings Institution Press, 2020.
6. Max Brooks et al., eds. *Strategy Strikes Back: How Star Wars Explains Modern Military Conflict*. With a foreword by Stanley McChrystal. Potomac Books, 2018.
7. Remo Pareschi et al., eds. *Human and Artificial Collaboration for Medical Best Practices*. Special issue. Frontiers in Human Dynamics, 2023.
8. Agni Orfanoudaki et al. "Algorithm, Human, or the Centaur: How to Enhance Clinical Care?" In: *HKS Working Paper No. RWP22-027* (2022). URL: https://scholar.harvard.edu/files/saghafian/files/centaur-web.pdf.
9. Remo Pareschi. "Abductive reasoning with the GPT-4 language model: Case studies from criminal investigation, medical practice, scientific research". In: *Sistemi intelligenti, Rivista quadrimestrale di scienze cognitive e di intelligenza artificiale* 2/2023 (2023), pp. 435–444. ISSN: 1120-9550. DOI: https://doi.org/10.1422/108139. URL: https://www.rivisteweb.it/doi/10.1422/108139.
10. Remo Pareschi and Federico Zappone. "Integrating Heuristics and Learning in a Computational Architecture for Cognitive Trading". In: *Artificial Intelligence and Financial Behaviour*. Ed. by Riccardo Viale et al. Edward Elgar Publishing, 2023, pp. 111–135. URL: https://www.elgaronline.com/edcollchap/book/9781803923154/book-part-9781803923154-12.xml.

Art and Artificial Intelligence Between Past, Present and Future

As we revisit our initial, most pressing concern—will artificial intelligence surpass human creativity in artistic endeavors?—it's crucial to recognize that the question, as commonly posed, is somewhat misdirected. Unlike games such as chess or Go, art cannot be measured by a simple win-lose metric. The fear, however, is similar: could humans be supplanted in artistic production as they have been in high-level chess?

Our analysis, grounded in cognitive considerations and carried out in the pages to come, suggests a nuanced answer. At the pinnacle of creativity—where inspiration, conception, and originality reign—AI is an enhancer, aiding in realizing powerful and original works. In such contexts, the human artist's role remains paramount, with AI serving as a tool to augment their creative vision. Conversely, AI's role can become more pronounced in domains where the creative demands are more structured or repetitive. It can automate the production of routine outputs such as certain types of commercial illustrations, brochures, or video game characters. This automation significantly impacts professionals in these fields, who may rely on such work for their livelihood. Consequently, these individuals may view the advent of AI technologies with apprehension and concern.[1]

Economic and Legal Implications

The economic threat of generative platforms is closely intertwined with concerns about copyright infringement. A notable legal action in this arena occurred in

[1] Similarly, the emergence of AI scripts and dialogues for movies and TV shows has sparked a debate in the entertainment industry. In 2022, the Writers Guild of America went on a strike to protest against using AI tools by major studios and networks, claiming they undermined writers' human creativity and labor. The strike lasted six months, resulting in a new collective bargaining agreement recognizing writers' rights and royalties concerning AI-generated content.

R. Pareschi, *Centaur Art*, https://doi.org/10.1007/978-3-031-69063-1_2

January 2023, when a group of artists filed a class-action lawsuit against Stability AI, Midjourney, and DeviantArt.[2] The lawsuit centered on the alleged unauthorized use of artists' works to train AI tools, sparking a debate over the legal and ethical boundaries of AI in art.

The highlighted lawsuit underscores the ongoing tension between AI's innovative potential in art and individual artists' rights. Plaintiffs in the case argued that AI tools were creating derivative works based on their styles without proper authorization or compensation. In contrast, the AI art companies defended their actions, asserting that the AI-generated images were transformative and original, thus not violating any laws. In a significant development in October 2023, a US judge dismissed most of these claims due to a lack of direct infringement evidence.[3]

On the other hand, to complicate matters further, the US Copyright Office in September 2023 rejected copyright protection for *Theatre D'opera Spatial*, an artwork predominantly created by AI and crafted by artist Jason Allen.[4] This artwork had previously won an art contest, but the Copyright Office's decision was based on the lack of significant human intervention in its creation. This stance contrasts with the position of Lawrence Lessig, a Harvard Law School professor and a renowned expert on Internet and law issues. Lessig advocates for the recognition of copyright in prompt-generated artworks, arguing that they are original and creative, embodying the human input of the prompter. He believes these works should be treated on par with other technologically aided art forms and that they have the potential to invigorate the art world by inspiring current artists and drawing in new audiences interested in AI's artistic capabilities.[5]

Interestingly, international perspectives on this issue vary. In November 2023, a Chinese court ruled that AI-generated content could be protected under copyright law, which starkly contrasts with the human authorship requirement under U.S. copyright law.[6]

Thus, despite these legal battles, the issue of copyright infringement in AI art remains unresolved, with the potential for future challenges and changes in various jurisdictions. This uncertainty underscores the evolving nature of art in the digital age and the need for a balanced approach that respects both innovation and artists' rights.

A striking example of the social impact of generative platforms is the publication of *Sunyata* by Eris Edizioni, an Italian graphic novel authored by philosopher and digital artist Francesco D'Isa that combines AI-generated images with traditional

---

[2] Source: https://arstechnica.com/tech-policy/2023/10/two-artists-suing-ai-image-makers-never-copyrighted-their-works/.

[3] Source: https://www.hollywoodreporter.com/business/business-news/artists-copyright-infringement-case-ai-art-generators-1235632929/.

[4] Source: https://www.reuters.com/legal/litigation/us-copyright-office-denies-protection-another-ai-created-image-2023-09-06/.

[5] Source: https://www.theverge.com/23929233/lawrence-lessig-free-speech-first-amendment-ai-content-moderation-decoder-interview.

[6] Source: https://www.jdsupra.com/legalnews/computer-love-beijing-court-finds-ai-7203152/.

text [1]. The novel ignited controversy among artists and comic book creators, who criticized its use of AI as undermining artistic integrity and economic fairness. The author and publisher defended their work as a legitimate artistic endeavor, emphasizing their careful use of prompts and adherence to a Creative Commons license.[7]

This case exemplifies the broader debate surrounding AI in art: balancing technological innovation with ethical considerations and the economic interests of human artists. As generative platforms continue to evolve, these discussions will likely intensify, shaping the future of art in the digital era. And yet, we might say that this is nothing new, with history repeating itself—the intersection of technology and art has always been a crucible of innovation and controversy.

Indeed, throughout history, technological advancements, from ink and paper to the development of cameras and computers, have continually opened new avenues for artistic expression. Yet, each technological leap has also brought ethical and social challenges, echoing today's tensions between generativity and control, authenticity and originality, and the impact of digital platforms on the art market.

Historically, resistance to new art forms and technologies is not a novel phenomenon but a recurring pattern. For instance, the advent of photography in the nineteenth century was initially met with skepticism by some critics and artists, who viewed it as a mechanical, uncreative process threatening traditional art forms. Similarly, introducing sound and color in cinema faced opposition, with concerns about diminishing the artistic value of silent and black-and-white films. Just as photography and color cinema once disrupted artistic norms, today's generative platforms like DALL-E, Stable Diffusion, and MidJourney are provoking similar debates in the art world.

To navigate this complex landscape, the insights of Walter Benjamin and John Maynard Keynes offer valuable perspectives. Benjamin was concerned about losing aura due to the mechanical reproduction of the work of art, but also recognized its democratizing potential. Generative platforms like DALL-E, Stable Diffusion, and MidJourney take this democratization one step further, making artistic creation more accessible and fostering a sense of community and creativity. Allowing users to generate and share art potentially fulfills Benjamin's social role in art.

While Benjamin's insights shed light on the cultural implications of technological advancements in art, John Maynard Keynes's concept of technological unemployment offers a crucial economic perspective. Among his many contributions to economic theory, Keynes, a prominent economist of the twentieth century, explored the job loss caused by technological advancements, a form of structural unemployment that he viewed as a 'temporary phase of maladjustment' [2]. This perspective is particularly relevant when considering the fears among artists about AI-powered generative platforms. While some artists worry about the potential for

[7] A Creative Commons license is a type of public copyright license that allows the author of a work to grant certain permissions to the public for using, sharing, and modifying the work while retaining some rights.

AI to diminish the demand for human-made art, thus impacting their livelihoods, it's crucial to recognize that technological changes can also create new job opportunities and artistic avenues.

Keynes' insights remind us that, despite initial disruptions, technological advancements often lead to the emergence of new roles and industries. In the context of art, generative AI might challenge traditional practices and pave the way for novel forms of artistic expression and collaboration. This evolution necessitates a redefinition of art and its creators, a task we aim to address in this book.

Historical Precedents in Artistic Innovation

Generative platforms are thus not only democratizing art but also making it more affordable and accessible. They lower the barriers to experimenting with AI in art, allowing a broader range of individuals to engage creatively. This democratization contrasts with the exclusive use of AI in art by well-resourced 'art moguls' like Damien Hirst, whose recent project *The Beautiful Paintings* capitalized on the opportunities presented by AI, generating significant financial returns. Thus, as we navigate the evolving landscape of art in the age of AI, we must consider both the challenges and the opportunities presented by these transformative technologies.

This is all the more relevant and challenging because generative AI transcends the role of a simple tool for image creation, like oil paint or Photoshop. It automates the creative process that, from an initial conception expressed in textual form, leads to its realization as digital content. This capability alone is insufficient to yield groundbreaking art, yet it provides a radically novel creation technique. We will show that this technique perfectly fits the centaur metaphor in an artistic context once combined with a human counterpart. Furthermore, an intriguing continuity with some aesthetic trends and artistic practices in the history of human art anticipates aspects of generative AI's creative process. These connections are worth exploring, as they can offer artists entry points to integrate this new method with their artistic practice.

Interestingly, this continuity turns out to be somewhat paradoxical. While the public worries about AI surpassing human abilities, various artistic communities and schools of thought have anticipated this development throughout history. We will briefly review some of these movements before delving into the algorithmic and computational mechanisms enabling machines to produce high-quality pictorial images. It's, however, crucial to note that, due to the complex and multifaceted nature of AI art implications, each artistic movement discussed pertains only to a portion of these aspects rather than their entirety.

Mannerism

Many centuries before the concept of artificial intelligence came into existence and computers were even invented, Mannerism, a multifaceted and diverse art movement, can be seen as a forerunner of the methods for creating visual content applied by today's generative platforms. Originally from Italy in the late fifteenth and early sixteenth centuries, Mannerism later spread to other European regions. Important Italian Mannerist artists include Giorgio Vasari, Rosso Fiorentino, Parmigianino, Jacopo Pontormo, Bronzino, Tintoretto, and Paolo Veronese. The movement further influenced artists like Francesco Primaticcio, El Greco, Bartholomeus Spranger, and Hendrick Goltzius in countries such as France, Spain, and the Netherlands.

Individual styles of Mannerist painters varied, yet they shared a common approach: to create new works of art based on existing ones rather than observing nature directly. Clearly, anti-naturalist approaches in art existed before and would reappear later. However, the Mannerist departure was specific by marking a shift towards elaboration and variation of pre-existing works. Mannerism can be seen as creative imitation or transformation, a process of reworking or reimagining previous art. Mannerist artists drew inspiration from past art, using it as a base for innovative works that challenged the boundaries of form, composition, and expression. They aimed to transcend conventions by taking traditional motifs, figures, themes, and compositions and elaborating or stylizing them in new ways or creating illusory or distorted spaces.

An interesting, albeit moderate, example of this way of making art is *The Wedding at Cana*[8] painted in 1563 by Paolo Veronese, the most important representative, together with Tintoretto, of the Venetian Mannerist school. This painting is based on the biblical story of Jesus turning water into wine at a wedding feast. In a bout of imaginative contamination, Veronese added many elements from contemporary Venetian society, such as musicians, animals, and exotic costumes. He also borrowed figures and poses from Raphael's frescoes in the Vatican and Michelangelo's Last Judgment in the Sistine Chapel.

Another is *The Burial of the Count of Orgaz*[9] by Domenikos Theotokópoulos, most widely known as El Greco, created between 1586 and 1588. This visionary Greek-born painter, active in Hapsburg sixteenth century Spain, was perhaps the Mannerist who most ostensibly influenced modern painters, including Pablo Picasso. This painting depicts a miraculous event that supposedly occurred in 1323, when two saints descended from heaven to bury a pious nobleman in Toledo, Spain. El Greco used his imagination and style to create a dramatic contrast between the earthly and heavenly realms and portray the faces and expressions of the local

[8] Source: https://www.louvre.fr/en/explore/the-palace/from-the-mona-lisa-to-the-wedding-feast-at-cana.

[9] Source: https://www.museodelprado.es/en/the-collection/art-work/the-burial-of-the-count-of-orgaz.

people who witnessed the event. He also incorporated some references to his Greek heritage, such as the Byzantine icons in the background.

Renowned among Mannerist artworks is the *Madonna with the Long Neck*,[10] created between 1534 and 1540 by Parmigianino, an Italian painter who also dabbled in magic and alchemy. This painting is one of the most famous examples of Mannerism, as it shows a distorted and exaggerated representation of the Virgin Mary and the Christ Child, with elongated limbs, small heads, and stylized features. Parmigianino was inspired by Michelangelo's sculptures, such as the Pietà and the Medici Madonna, but also added some elements of his invention, such as the mysterious column and the unfinished group of angels on the right.

In parallel, generative AI draws from existing art, manipulating and merging elements to craft novel creations. Both methods involve using existing works as inspiration and reference and applying creative modifications and combinations to produce new and original images. However, there are also some important differences between the two methods. The Mannerist artists were influenced by the artistic styles and techniques of the Renaissance masters, such as Michelangelo, Raphael, and Leonardo da Vinci. They often imitated their compositions, proportions, and perspectives but exaggerated and distorted them to create a sense of tension, drama, and emotion. As we will see when delving into the technology of generative AI, the generating platforms, on the other hand, are trained on a large and diverse dataset of text-image pairs, which may include various genres, styles, and themes. They do not necessarily follow specific artistic rules or conventions but generate images consistent with text descriptions and hidden patterns.

Even more crucially, the Mannerist artists were aware of their creative process and artistic choices. They had a conscious intention and purpose behind their paintings, such as expressing their vision, challenging the norms, or pleasing their patrons. The AI-generating platforms, however, are not conscious or intentional. They are driven by mathematical algorithms and statistical methods that optimize for certain objectives, such as likelihood, diversity, or realism. They do not have any intrinsic meaning or value behind their images other than satisfying the input query.

More than anything else, the Mannerist artists were subject to emotions and experiences and were influenced by their cultural backgrounds. They also interacted with other artists and audiences who could appreciate, critique, or interpret their paintings. The AI-generating platforms are artificial systems without emotions, experiences, or cultural backgrounds affecting their images. Nor do they interact with other systems or humans who can appreciate, critique, or interpret such works.

These differences notwithstanding, by tapping into the shared theme of reimagining existing works, contemporary artists can harness the capabilities of generative platforms in a neo-mannerist fashion by letting platforms generate images according to a certain style or referring to a very specific painting or painter and then, through manual intervention, adding to it the human side, namely intentions, emotions, concepts, and meanings.

[10] Source: https://www.uffizi.it/en/artworks/parmigianino-madonna-long-neck.

In the late sixteenth century, Baroque eventually replaced Mannerism, whose innovative approach had given life to a type of art ahead of its time. Baroque art reintroduced the classical point of view under the new guise of realism. Mannerism's pioneering contributions had to wait until the early twentieth century for recognition. Its anticipatory modes of expression found echoes in avant-garde movements such as Surrealism, Futurism, and Expressionism, which played an important role in rediscovering and appreciating its innovative modes.[11] Using AI technology, contemporary artists can also experiment with creative approaches, techniques, and distortions of previous works, potentially ushering in a neo-mannerist season.

Surrealist Automation

A gap of roughly 400 years separates Mannerism from the next antecedents of AI-powered art. Among these, all of which emerged during the first half of the twentieth century, Surrealism explicitly and systematically explored the automation of artistic creation.

Surrealist artists turned to the human mind as the source for automated artistic creation. André Breton, a French poet and writer regarded as the movement's founder, defined Surrealism in his 1924 Surrealist Manifesto [6] as 'pure psychic automatism,' which aimed to express 'the real functioning of thought.' Surrealists employed automatism to tap into the unconscious mind, revealing latent aspects of human nature, such as the hidden self and its deepest desires and fears. Techniques such as automatic writing and free association were used to bypass conscious control and access the subconscious.

Not limited to the written word, automatism also found its way into visual arts, particularly painting. Salvador Dalí, for instance, employed a method he called the 'paranoiac-critical method,' a form of active imagination that allowed him to tap into subconscious associations and imagery. His paintings, like *The Persistence of Memory*,[12] are iconic examples of how automatism can manifest visually, incorporating dream-like scenes and irrational juxtapositions.

---

[11] Mannerism's connection with twentieth-century artistic movements has been analyzed in notable studies. Key works include John Shearman's Mannerism [3], Sidney J. Freedberg's Painting of the High Renaissance and Mannerism in Rome and Central Italy [4], and Hellmut Wohl's The Aesthetics of Italian Renaissance Art: A Reconsideration of Style [5]. Pablo Picasso is perhaps the best-known twentieth-century artist influenced by Mannerism. His study of various past masters includes Mannerist artists, and this influence is evident in his works. Salvador Dalí's style also resembles Mannerism, particularly in his elongated figures and complex spaces. While Dalí never explicitly linked his work to Mannerism, art historians have noted the connection. Giorgio de Chirico's metaphysical paintings and Egon Schiele's contorted body shapes also draw comparisons to Mannerist art.

[12] Source: https://www.moma.org/collection/works/79018.

Max Ernst utilized *frottage* (rubbing) and *grattage* (scraping) techniques to create textured paintings that served as a canvas for exploring unconscious imagery. His works often started as random textures, from which he would 'discover' hidden images, much like one might find shapes in clouds or patterns in nature.

Joan Miró used automatism to free his art from traditional techniques and conscious control. His works often started as doodles or 'automatic drawings,' which he would later transform into complex paintings. René Magritte, on the other hand, used surreal automatism to challenge perceptions of reality, creating paintings that juxtaposed everyday objects in unexpected ways.

During the second phase of Surrealism, also known as Verism, artists shifted focus to more realistic depictions yet still emphasized the connection to the subconscious. This phase saw the use of hyper-realistic techniques to create dream-like, yet lifelike, images that further blurred the line between the conscious and the unconscious.

Generative AI could create new possibilities for artistic expression by combining writing and visual arts based on the Surrealist principles. Automatic writing techniques could produce prompts to create images with AI platforms that innovatively relate words and visuals to reflect the human mind.

Cubism

In the early twentieth century, before the advent of Surrealism and preceding the First World War, Cubism emerged in France as a revolutionary artistic movement and one of the first significant contributions to modern art. The movement's primary pioneers were Pablo Picasso and Georges Braque, whose *Les Demoiselles d'Avignon*[13] (1907) and *Houses at L'Estaque*[14] (1908), respectively, are among the earliest and most influential examples of Cubist art. Fragmented, abstract forms and the representation of multiple viewpoints characterize these works. Cubism sought to deconstruct reality by intersecting objective geometric shapes with the artist's subjective perspective, challenging conventional representations of objects and allowing for innovative interpretations.

Cubism's momentum in purely geometrical terms waned as the possibilities within Euclidean geometry, the framework in which Cubist artists operated, became fully explored. The movement's innovative spirit found new expression in post-World War I avant-garde movements, such as Surrealism. However, AI-based art could revive and extend the original geometric program of Cubism by pursuing more complex and radical forms of geometric abstraction. AI algorithms can generate geometric shapes and patterns that go beyond the limitations of Euclidean geometry. For instance, they may use topology, non-Euclidean geometries such as hyperbolic and elliptical, and fractal models to create geometric abstractions at various scales.

[13] Source: https://www.moma.org/collection/works/79766.

[14] Source: https://en.wikipedia.org/wiki/Houses_at_l%27Estaque.

These geometric forms, precisely because they are alternatives to the familiarity of Euclidean geometry, are intriguing from the standpoint of artistic innovation. Moreover, their use in scientific contexts for visualizing complex data patterns has proven highly effective. These unconventional yet revealing perspectives can be generated through textual prompts provided as input to generative platforms; afterward, they can be evolved by adding pictorial contributions to the images produced by artificial intelligence. This process reinterprets the original Cubist program under the umbrella of a broader 'geometrism.'

Kandinsky and Abstract Expressionism

If Cubists rigorously analyzed and deconstructed painted subjects into geometric shapes, Abstract Expressionists explored large abstract spaces characterized by either flat calm, as exemplified by Mark Rothko, or material chaos, as in Jackson Pollock's work. The movement emerged in the United States in the 1940s, heavily influenced by Russian-born, French-naturalized artist Wassily Kandinsky, a major innovator of the early twentieth century. Kandinsky's works often evoke cosmic spatiality and astral landscapes.

Though Kandinsky's sublime achievements influenced future generations of abstract expressionists, his creativity could have been further stimulated by moving beyond the naked-eye perception of space and incorporating astonishing images from the most remote parts of the universe captured by modern telescopes, as well as simulations of relativistic and quantum phenomena like wormholes and quantum entanglements.[15] With its vast data repositories and content creation capabilities, generative AI makes this wealth of cosmic imagery accessible, paving the way for expanding Kandinsky's approach on a grander cosmic scale.

Mathematical and Computational Art

Artificial intelligence employs mathematical and computational methods to generate art. Before its advent, some envisioned a type of art based on mathematical and

[15] An abundance of breathtaking images from the farthest reaches of the universe, captured by the most advanced telescopes, are available in repositories like those provided by NASA. These fascinating visuals have been incorporated into the training data for generative AI platforms, which can also resort to cinematic portrayals of complex yet unobserved phenomena, such as the wormholes in the movie "Interstellar," or graphic representations of quantum entanglement (e.g., by representing two interconnected particles with lines that indicate properties like spin or polarization) for image creation.

Source: https://www.jpl.nasa.gov/news/nasa-reveals-webb-telescopes-first-images-of-unseen-universe, https://solarsystem.nasa.gov/missions/hubble-space-telescope/in-depth/.

computational principles. Some artists had resorted to mathematical production principles as early as the beginning of the twentieth century.

The Dutch De Stijl movement, founded in the Netherlands in 1917, and its most renowned representative, Piet Mondrian, viewed art as a derivative of mathematics and geometry. De Stijl aimed to create a universal visual language by reducing elements to their most basic forms, like lines, squares, and primary colors, promoting harmony and balance through simple geometric shapes and a limited color palette. De Stijl influenced various artistic disciplines, including painting, furniture design, and architecture, seeking to contribute to a better world through simplicity and order, according to formats accessible to everyone regardless of cultural background. This vision significantly influenced other artistic movements, like the Bauhaus in Germany, and remains an essential reference for those interested in the intersection of form, color, and space. Mondrian's abstract compositions, featuring rectangular blocks of color separated by thin black lines, strictly adhere to geometric principles and a limited color palette.

By contrast, Maurits Escher, a Dutch artist slightly later than De Stijl, used mathematics and geometry to create complex and paradoxical art. Cognitive scientist Douglas Hofstadter covered Escher extensively in his 1979 bestseller *Gödel, Escher, Bach: an Eternal Golden Braid* [7], devoted to artificial intelligence's logical and philosophical implications. Escher's work features tessellations and impossible geometrical objects, which Hofstadter argues are visual representations of paradoxes and self-referential structures in mathematical and computational systems. Escher's graphics can also be considered a visual analog of musical patterns and structures, making his work particularly relevant to AI-based content generation.

The Op Art movement, founded by Hungarian-born French artist Victor Vasarely, also placed mathematics at the core of figurative content creation. Op Art uses optical illusions, patterns, repetition, and color and form manipulation to create visually dynamic works that appear to move or change when viewed. Vasarely and other Op Art artists explored the relationship between form, color, and perception. They often utilized mathematical algorithms and geometric shapes to create works that challenged the viewers' perception and engaged their eyes in a dynamic dialogue with their minds. Op Art can be seen as a form of visual mathematics, using mathematical and geometric principles to investigate the nature of perception and the relationship between the mind and the external world. The connection between Op Art and computation is more indirect, yet it emerges in manipulating visual elements, which aligns with the fundamental principles of computer graphics and animation.

Arte Programmata, emerging in Italy in the 1960s, used computer programming and algorithms to create dynamic and interactive works. Artists like Bruno Munari, a key figure in this movement, used mechanical devices, light, and sound to create interactive, kinetic, and dynamic artworks. Munari's work, such as *Munari's Machine* (1956) and *Macchina Aritmica* (1951), combined abstract-geometric forms with computer technology, adding a political and social dimension to his art. Arte Programmata shared similarities with Op Art in stimulating viewer perception but differed in its use of computer technology to create more complex and immersive experiences.

Andy Warhol and the Mass Production of Works of Art

Algorithmic art production through AI platforms introduces a high degree of automation to the creative process. A relevant precursor is Andy Warhol, who pioneered mass-produced artwork through his concept of the 'factory.' Initially, the Factory was Warhol's studio, a creative space where he collaborated with artists and musicians. Warhol later extended the concept to mass production techniques like photo-silkscreen, creating iconic pop art pieces such as portraits of Marilyn Monroe and Elvis Presley and paintings of Campbell's Soup Cans and Coca-Cola bottles. The art factory challenged traditional notions of artistic creation, integrated different art forms, and concretized Warhol's focus on mass culture, celebrity, and commercialism.

AI-powered art aligns with the art factory concept through its potential to automate and mass-produce art. However, it also pushes the boundaries of artistic creation and experimentation beyond traditional mass production constraints. AI-powered art combines mass production with individualized expression by automating artwork production and enabling artists to explore new forms of expression and generate innovative designs through algorithms. Realizing this potential would merge the best of both worlds, increasing automation while maintaining a high degree of individual creativity.

These considerations fittingly conclude this chapter, tying back to Walter Benjamin's ideas on the mechanical reproduction of art. Benjamin hypothesized that mechanical reproduction might lead to losing art's unique and original qualities tied to physical presence. AI-powered art solves this impasse by combining the creation of unique and original pieces through algorithmic processes with their easy reproduction and distribution. This updates Benjamin's concept to a world where art can be mass-produced while retaining individual creative qualities.

References

1. Francesco D'Isa. *Sunyata*. Eris Edizioni, 2023.
2. John Maynard Keynes. "Economic possibilities for our grandchildren". In: *Essays in persuasion* 9 (1930), pp. 358–373.
3. John Shearman. *Mannerism*. Penguin Books, 1967.
4. Sidney J. Freedberg. *Painting of the High Renaissance and Mannerism in Rome and Central Italy*. Penguin Books, 1971.

5. Hellmut Wohl. *The Aesthetics of Italian Renaissance Art: A Reconsideration of Style*. Cambridge University Press, 1999.
6. André Breton. *The Manifesto of Surrealism*. Trans. by Richard Seaver and Helen R. Lane. Translated from the French by Richard Seaver and Helen R. Lane. Original version: Breton, André. Manifeste du surréalisme. Paris: Éditions du Sagittaire, 1924. University of Michigan Press, 1969.
7. Douglas R. Hofstadter. *Gödel, Escher, Bach: An Eternal Golden Braid*. Twentieth Anniversary Edition. Basic Books, 1999.

AI for Games and Art

This chapter delves into the conceptual foundations that underlie artificial intelligence's role in game-playing and art creation. The previous chapters argued for humans' contrasting roles in centaur systems designed for these distinct realms. However, it's essential to recognize that the core architecture of the artificial components in both settings is remarkably similar. What differentiates them is their influence and the functions they serve within the broader system.

AI has become very proficient in strategic games, surpassing human capabilities in complex perfect information games such as chess and Go. Conversely, AI acts as a catalyst for innovation in the artistic sphere, enhancing rather than supplanting human creativity. This pattern isn't coincidental; it can be generalized across various systems that bear resemblances to both games and art. As we'll explore, this divergence stems from the fundamental difference between closed and open systems.

By delving into the mechanisms that underlie the role of artificial intelligence in strategy games and artistic activities, we can also define realistic terms of comparison with human creativity. Just as generative AI operates based on probabilistic algorithms and rules, human artists, over time, internalize certain norms and standards of artistic creation. These ingrained "rules" guide their creative expressions, practiced almost machine-like in their adherence. In essence, even without a generative platform, artists often resort to a systematic component deeply rooted in their creative psyche.

AI for Games

A driving force behind these developments is the MinMax algorithm. Although simple, it has fueled the evolution of artificial players from early attempts at artificial intelligence to Deep Blue, which defeated Garry Kasparov in 1997, and its successors like Stockfish, which have long since insurmountably surpassed all

R. Pareschi, *Centaur Art*, https://doi.org/10.1007/978-3-031-69063-1_3

human players. MinMax also plays a significant role in artificial intelligence-based content generation.

First proposed by John von Neumann and Oskar Morgenstern in their 1944 book *The Theory of Games and Economic Behavior* [1], the MinMax algorithm determines the best move for a player in an n-player, zero-sum game. In game theory, a zero-sum game is a situation in which other players' loss precisely balances one player's gain, maintaining a constant amount of wealth, resources, or utility. Examples of zero-sum games include chess, poker, and other games where one player's winnings come at the expense of the other.

Zero-sum games can be classified into two types: perfect information games and imperfect information games. In the first type, which includes chess, checkers, and tic-tac-toe, players fully know the game's state and their opponents' actions. The situation is reversed in the other type, which includes poker, stratego, and battleship.

MinMax is primarily applied to two-player, zero-sum games with alternating moves and perfect information. It is less suited for games with imperfect information, where it struggles to account for uncertainty and hidden variables. In perfect information games like tic-tac-toe, checkers, and chess, each player moves in turn, and MinMax chooses the best move for each player each turn. The algorithm explores the possible moves for the player who has to move, starting from the assumption that the other player will not discount, i.e., they will always respond with the most unfavorable countermove. Faced with the other player's supposed countermove, the current player selects the move that gives them the greatest advantage. MinMax looks for moves traversing a tree structure where the branches of each node represent the alternatives. It analyzes the game in progress, going as deep as possible and evaluating the longest sequences of moves. A graphical representation of this process is given in Fig. 1, where the root node labeled 'Max' represents the maximizing player's decision; the nodes labeled 'Min' represent the minimizing player's decision; the leaf nodes contain the utility values for the maximizing player. The maximizing player aims to maximize the utility value, while the minimizing player aims to minimize it. The tree is traversed to find the optimal move for the maximizing player. It is located in this specific tree at its rightmost extremity, corresponding to the 'worst best move' possible for the minimizing player.

The diagram in Fig. 1 represents a simplified MinMax tree, which is only one-ply deep. In game theory and computer science, a 'ply' refers to one move by one player. Therefore, a one-ply tree only considers the immediate next moves without looking further ahead. In real-world applications, especially in complex games like chess, MinMax trees can reach arbitrary depths depending on the computational resources available. Current chess engines, for example, can analyze well beyond 20 plys, considering numerous possible future scenarios before making a move. The depth to which the tree is explored is often limited by the memory and processing power of the player, whether human or artificial. The deeper the tree, the more accurate the decision-making will be. However, this depth also demands more computational resources to analyze. Thus, the depth of a MinMax tree is a crucial factor that can significantly impact the quality of the game strategy, and it can vary widely depending on the capabilities of the entity employing it.

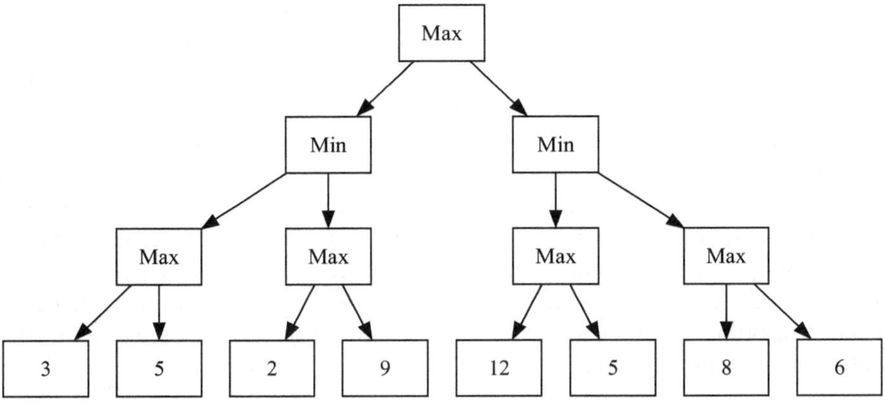

Fig. 1 MinMax game tree

MinMax always finds the best move in simple games like tic-tac-toe. This fact, together with the limited number of positions that can be created, has made it possible to demonstrate that in tic-tac-toe, the perfect game by both leads to a draw, thus making it a solved game. A game is solved when a strategy guarantees one player to win or, if all players play perfectly, it results in a tie. In the case of zero-sum games for two players, this means that there is a strategy that one player can always use to beat any opponent or that both players can use perfect play to ensure that the game always ends in a draw.

Despite the success in solving some zero-sum games, not all have been conquered. The most complex game solved to date is checkers, cracked in 2007 by a University of Alberta team that developed Chinook, as reported in [2]. This program utilized a 39 trillion endgame positions database and 200 desktop computers. Chinook proved that perfect play always results in a draw with a search space of 5×10^{20} positions. However, chess and Go present significantly greater challenges, with generable positions of 10^{120} and 10^{174}, respectively. To emphasize the magnitude, the number of positions in chess alone surpasses the estimated number of atoms in the universe.

Consequently, solving these games with algorithms like MinMax on conventional computers remains out of reach. Claude Shannon, a twentieth-century mathematician known for his ground-breaking contributions to information theory, estimated that solving chess would take 1019 years.[1]

[1] In an article published in 1950 [3], Shannon estimated 1019 years to solve chess based on the computational power available at that time. Since then, computational capabilities have advanced significantly, and the development of AI and machine learning techniques have improved how we approach solving complex problems like chess. However, despite these advancements, solving chess completely remains a challenge. The number of possible positions in chess is approximately 10^{120}, which, as we indicated above, is an extremely large number. Indeed, although modern chess engines like Stockfish and AlphaZero have demonstrated super-human performance and are far

Once reliable and stable, quantum computers could bring significant progress in solving chess, as suggested by Jonathan Schaeffer, who led the team that solved checkers. For now, we must be content with conjectures backed by statistics. Two plausible alternative conjectures are: (1) since the percentage of draws in chess games played by top human or artificial players consistently exceeds 50%, perfect play likely ends in a draw; (2) most wins are achieved by white, and most of them using the queen's pawn opening, suggesting that perfect play could result in a win for white if employing this strategy. Game engine pioneer and chess champion Hans Berliner supported the second conjecture, as described in his book *The System: A World Champion's Approach to Chess* [4]. He meant to prove it mathematically without resorting to brute force search. Unfortunately, he passed away in 2017 without completing the project.

MinMax-Based Chess Engines

While methods like MinMax have not solved chess, they have allowed artificial players to surpass human performance definitively and unassailably. Despite psychological studies on how expert human players make sophisticated decisions and numerous treatises on chess strategy, the seemingly simplistic approach of MinMax has proven effective. Several factors have contributed to this success, not least of which is the exponential progress of computer hardware. Gordon Moore, one of the founders of semiconductor giant Intel, formulated the law, which has proven reliable, according to which the number of transistors on a microchip doubles every 2 years while their cost halves. Consequently, computers' speed and capacity increase exponentially over time, and their cost decreases.[2] While there are no specific studies on the correlation between Moore's Law and the progress of artificial chess players, some connection seems quite apparent. In 1957, Herbert Simon, a Nobel Prize winner and one of the "founding fathers" of artificial intelligence, predicted that artificial chess players would surpass humans in 10 years. This forecast was met with skepticism, as many believed that chess was too complex for computers. However, Simon's prediction proved accurate, albeit

more efficient than brute-force searching, they still need to solve the game. In summary, while Shannon's original estimate of 1019 years might not be accurate with today's computational power, completely solving chess is still a monumental challenge.

[2] A recent evolution of Moore's law is Huang's law, named after Nvidia CEO Jensen Huang, which describes how graphics processing units (GPUs) performance more than doubles every 2 years. GPUs are processing units highly specialized for tasks like video gaming, mining of cryptocurrencies, and AI applications like machine learning. Huang's law is enabled by Moore's law but also by advances in architecture, interconnects, memory technology, and algorithms. Huang's law suggests that GPUs are becoming more important than central processing units (CPUs) for many computing tasks, such as machine learning, gaming, and graphics.

Source: https://cacm.acm.org/news/247515uangs-law-is-the-new-moores-law-and-explains-why-nvid-hia-wants-arm/fulltext.

delayed by 30 years. Moore's Law, formulated 8 years after the prophecy, could have helped him be more precise.[3]

Paralleling the growth of computational power in line with Moore's Law, MinMax has also been optimized and refined, leading artificial players to outperform their human counterparts with consistently growing performance gaps. A widely used refinement is Alpha-Beta pruning. In MinMax, a player seeks to make the best move, assuming that the opponent behaves the same and analyzing sequences of moves and countermoves as deeply as memory permits. Alpha-Beta pruning improves on this method by eliminating moves from evaluation if at least one countermove is better to the opponent than a previously considered move.

To grasp how Alpha-Beta pruning works, consider a simple 2-player game where each player has bags containing items with different values, and both are aware of the contents of the bags of the other. In each round, a coin toss determines who receives a prize from the opponent's bags. The receiver chooses the bag, and the giver chooses the item to give. The first bag contains an opera ticket, a sandwich, and 20 euros; in a MinMax scenario, the opponent will choose the sandwich. The second bag includes a fishbone and other items, such as a gold bar, a dinner-for-two coupon at a starred restaurant, and a 5000 euro prepaid card. The opponent will choose the bone since it is advantageous compared to the sandwich, while all other options are worse. Consequently, there is no need to look further, and the option provided by the second bag is pruned.

Applied to a MinMax tree, Alpha-Beta optimization returns the same moves as MinMax but eliminates branches that do not affect the final decision. This frees up computational resources that can be used to explore relevant alternatives in more depth. Further refinement comes from combining MinMax with iterative deepening, a technique originally designed to handle searching across infinite domains. Even if a solution to a problem exists within a search space of this kind, a computational engine may not find it if engaged in an infinite branch unless redirected to a branch containing the solution. Iterative deepening solves this problem by progressively extending the search depth: $1, 2, \ldots, n$. This allows for finding solutions at arbitrary depths and breadths, as a search engine engaged in an infinite branch must abandon it to move to another branch once the current depth level is reached; if no solution is found within the current depth, this is increased by one and the search restarts from scratch. The computational cost of this process, a consequence of repeating and extending the search every time the depth level is updated, is offset by the guarantee of finding a solution. Iterative deepening also proves effective in search domains that, while finite, are extremely large, such as chess. Without iterative deepening, a MinMax engine, even if Alpha-Beta-optimized, would explore branches individually, going as deep as possible given the

[3] More than 30 years later than Simon's prophecy, Ray Kurzweil, the well-known futurist, also ventured into predicting in his 1990 bestselling book, *The Age of Intelligent Machines* [5], that a computer would defeat a chess champion of the world by 1998. This time the prediction ended up exact.

computational resources available. Instead, with iterative deepening, it might find that the best move is, say, at level 3 of a branch and stop there. Therefore, iterative deepening may prove crucial in enhancing game performance with time constraints (for example, 40 moves per player within 2 hours), thus saving computational resources for use when necessary.

MinMax, Alpha-Beta pruning, and the various search strategies, from straightforward depth-first search to iterative deepening, are effective only when paired with a reliable evaluation function to choose between alternatives. An evaluation function helps discard losing choices, as illustrated in the bags-of-prizes game example used to demonstrate Alpha-Beta pruning. Evaluation functions are relatively straightforward for elementary games like tic-tac-toe since the MinMax tree can traverse all viable alternatives, leading to only three outcomes: draw, victory, or defeat. However, in the case of chess, the situation is considerably more complex. The immense, albeit finite, search space dimensions prevent any human or artificial player from fully exploring all available alternatives at the game's start. Until a winning position for either player or a theoretical draw.[4] arises, the search process must stop at some point, with several playable positions to choose from after pruning the worst cases using Alpha-Beta. This is where more advanced aspects of an evaluation function are of the essence, such as assessing the material value on the board, piece positioning, and defensive vulnerabilities. For example, the knight and bishop generally have a value between 3 and 3.5, with the weight of a pawn serving as the basic unit of 1. The game context determines how much these values can vary within these limits. A knight may assume higher values in closed game situations, characterized by pawn chains, due to its ability to bypass them; this context penalizes the bishop, which conversely gains value in open game situations because of its broader range of action compared to the knight. Similarly, a pawn's weight can fluctuate from the primary value of 1 depending on whether it is doubled with another pawn—devaluing both pawns due to their inability to defend each other—or passed, increasing its value because the opponent pawns cannot obstruct its advancement.

The refinement of evaluation functions in chess is limited only by the computational resources, which have been continually improving due to Moore's Law. The most sophisticated MinMax engines evaluate positions by considering hundreds of features, e.g., each with its specific weight, based on criteria defined by their development teams and supported by experienced human players. As a result, humans still contribute to the evolution of strategy games, primarily through designing and providing technical assistance to chess engines. These engines can vary in decision-making and playstyles depending on how their rating features are

[4] "Theoretical draw" situations are those where the game is guaranteed to end in a draw if both players play perfectly. Thus, these situations define a chess subset that can be considered solved, itself part of a larger solved subset, which includes all positions with seven or fewer pieces on the board. For these positions, it is known whether perfect play leads to a draw or the win of one of the players.

designed and implemented. However, they converge when playing "by the book," selecting the best moves according to chess theory.

While AI players now outperform humans, their introduction has, paradoxically, led to significant growth in the chess community. Interest in chess and other strategy games has surged at all levels. At the grassroots, there's been a boom in online players. At the elite level, collaborations have formed between professional players, software engineers, computer scientists, and research labs, all pushing the boundaries of technology. Developers have not only crafted advanced chess engines but have also transformed correspondence chess with intuitive interfaces for PCs, tablets, and smartphones. Platforms like the International Correspondence Chess Confederation (ICCF) and the Free Internet Correspondence Game Server (FICGS) have made chess widely accessible online. Websites such as chess.com and Lichess have expanded local chess communities to a global scale, with more individuals playing online against both AI and human opponents. With its enforced lockdowns, the 2020–2023 Covid pandemic further boosted this trend by offering an engaging pastime for those confined to their homes. Thus, the paradox lies in that while AI has surpassed human performance in chess, its entry into the scene has broadened and democratized the game's reach. We posit that a similar trend will emerge in the art community. However, unlike chess, the pinnacle of artistic creativity will remain untouched by AI due to the intrinsic differences between art and strategy games.

Chess Engines Based on Neural Networks

Meanwhile, at the top of the broadened chess community, where chess engines relentlessly push the performance envelope, a momentous shift has occurred with the emergence of a potent alternative to MinMax engines: neural networks.

On December 5th, 2017, about 20 years after Deep Blue's victory over Kasparov, DeepMind, a subsidiary of Google, announced AlphaZero, a chess engine developed based on machine learning—a technology entirely different from that of MinMax engines [6]. Starting from its initial training phase, AlphaZero achieved superhuman skill levels in chess, Shogi, and Go within 24 hours of machine learning operations. This rapid advancement allowed it to surpass the remarkable achievements of its predecessor, AlphaGoZero, which had previously bested human champions in the game of Go. In a much-publicized event, AlphaZero challenged Stockfish, the leading MinMax engine, and emerged victorious, winning 25 games as white, three as black, and drawing the remaining 72. Although the results were impressive, it's important to note that the playing conditions for Stockfish were not ideal. All games were played with a fixed time limit of 1 minute per move, preventing Stockfish from effectively utilizing its time management strategies. In standard chess tournament conditions, such as 40 moves in 2 hours, players strategically allocate their time based on the complexity and critical nature of the moves. The imposition of a fixed time per move significantly handicapped Stockfish's performance. Moreover, the version of Stockfish used in the match was not the latest, and analysis of the games suggested that the competition would have been more evenly matched had an updated Stockfish been used under standard conditions. Other MinMax engines like Komodo and Houdini would also have presented significant challenges. Subsequent matches have demonstrated a closer balance between neural network-based and MinMax engines. Despite these considerations, the 2017 demonstration by AlphaZero marked a historical turning point, showcasing the potent application capabilities of neural networks in chess and other strategic games.

Neural networks, the key technology behind AlphaZero and similar engines, are algorithms designed to identify patterns and make predictions from vast data. They do not depend on predefined rules or search methods but on their ability to learn from experience and adapt to new situations. Chess engines like AlphaZero employ a form of reinforcement learning, where an agent trains by interacting with the environment and receiving rewards or penalties for its actions. The goal is to learn behavior that maximizes rewards over time. A common application of reinforcement learning is training experimental autonomous vehicles, such as self-driving cars or drones, by exposing them to various scenarios and allowing them to learn through trial and error. This process simulates the vehicle's environment, including road conditions, traffic, and potential obstacles. The vehicle takes actions in response to these stimuli and receives rewards or penalties based on how closely its actions align with the desired behavior. Over time, it learns which actions are most likely to yield positive results and adapts its behavior accordingly, enabling it to navigate and cope with diverse scenarios. Reinforcement learning also applies to contexts like chessboard strategy games, which are far removed from the physical circumstances of driving on the road. In AlphaZero's case, the agent plays millions of games against itself, learning from experience. AlphaZero utilizes a deep learning network composed of multiple layers of interconnected neurons that process and analyze information, enhancing its capabilities. This allows it to recognize complex patterns and make more sophisticated decisions than single-layer neural networks.

Due to differences in design and decision-making processes, chess engines based on neural networks and MinMax technology can exhibit different playing styles. Engines like AlphaZero, which rely on neural networks, often display a more intuitive and riskier style of play. Their training allows them to develop a nuanced and flexible approach to the game, resulting in more intuitive and unpredictable moves.[5] MinMax-based engines like Stockfish systematically explore the game tree and evaluate moves using pre-set rules, which leads to a more predictable and logical yet less intuitive and flexible style of play. These differences in playing style are reflected in the preparation of the two types of artificial players: training with data for neural networks and evaluation criteria for reached positions and other heuristics devised by a team of chess experts and software developers for MinMax engines.

[5] This flexibility and risk-taking attitude makes neural network-based engines also well-suited for games with imperfect information, where the state of the game is partially hidden or uncertain, such as Poker, Stratego, and Battleship. Witness the superhuman performance of engines like DeepNash in Stratego [7].

Thinking Fast and Slow

MinMax has its roots in game theory, with applications ranging from strategy games to economics, while neural networks originate from machine learning. They represent decision-making systems realized, respectively, through "decision through reasoning" and "decision through learning." MinMax explicitly reasons by evaluating options to choose the best move. Alpha-Beta optimization serves as meta-reasoning, allowing the player to move on to the next option if the current one is worse than those examined earlier.

To understand the applicability of these two decision-making modes in the artificial and human domains, consider driving a car and planning investments. The ability to drive safely and effectively arises from innate qualities and experience. Learning is the only way to evolve these natural dispositions into effective skills through initial supervision and subsequent independent practice. On the other hand, planning investment is about going beyond mere experience; careful reasoning about choices and decisions becomes essential.

In human decision-making, Daniel Kahneman, a Nobel Prize-winning economist, differentiates between fast and slow thinking.[6] Fast thinking operates through learned automatisms, as happens when driving, while slow thinking relies on careful and reasoned considerations, as in investment planning. However, Kahneman also highlights surprising situations where fast thinking is employed when slow thinking would be expected and vice versa.

Recently, some AI researchers have looked to dual-process theory to inform the development of AI systems, explicitly integrating elements of fast and slow thinking.[7] By contrast, we adopt the perspective that high-performance systems—including leading chess engines and generative AIs—demonstrate the co-occurrence of fast and slow thinking, even if it may not have been an intentional design feature but a byproduct of designs aimed at complex environments. We will begin exploring game engines before turning our attention to generative AI. A crucial disclaimer is that our use of the term "thinking" concerning machines is purely functional, in that we refer thus to the ability to perform tasks that simulate human cognitive processes, in line with how Alan Turing used the term in his foundational essay, *Computing Machinery and Intelligence* [11]. This approach sidesteps deeper philosophical questions around consciousness and intentionality typically associated with human thought.

[6] This distinction, the fruit of decades of field research, is systematically addressed by Kahneman in his bestselling book *Thinking, Fast and Slow* [8].

[7] Booch et al. in *Thinking Fast and Slow in AI* [9] have proposed a research direction that involves embedding cognitive components—such as metacognition, self-awareness, and causal reasoning—within AI systems. They put forth a multi-agent architecture where distinct agents can engage in either fast or slow thinking, depending on the task and context. Building on this, Ganapini et al. in *Thinking Fast and Slow in AI: the Role of Metacognition* [10] introduced a world model and a self-model to support both agents. They delved into how metacognition can assist AI systems in monitoring and regulating their cognitive processes.

In strategy games, artificial agents can operate in fast or slow thinking methods; both have their merits and are workable, but neither is perfect, as both encounter limitations regarding the ideal situations for exclusively applying one way of thinking over the other. MinMax exemplifies slow thinking by systematically evaluating the best move step by step. However, it must contend with temporal limitations, such as the time allotted for a chess match, and constraints on computational resources. To tackle these challenges, which bring its application conditions closer to those of fast thinking, MinMax uses optimizations like Alpha-Beta pruning, iterative deepening, and heuristic evaluation for intermediate positions. On the other hand, methods based on neural networks treat the choice of the best move with the level of spontaneity and automatism with which one drives a car. However, this approach must be tempered when evaluating a position based on multiple criteria, which must be explicitly weighable and quantifiable, as would occur in investment planning or building design. To manage situations where recourse to experience is insufficient, neural networks like AlphaZero are integrated with decision-making methods such as Monte Carlo Tree Search (MCTS). MCTS uses random sampling to estimate the value of different actions and selects the action with the highest estimated value. This systematic and logical process is a form of slow thinking, as it adheres to a structured and deliberate approach to decision-making.

AI for Art

Moving from strategy games to the field of art, we will see how AI-based art imitates the creative process of human artists, harmonizing the quick spark of intuition with the meticulous cycle of revisions and refinements seen in great works. This principle seems to apply across the artistic spectrum, from classical art, where the work evolves from the initial sketch to the final result, to abstract conceptual art, where multiple attempts may be needed to manifest the concept poignantly and effectively.

Generative Adversarial Networks

An artist might start the work with fluid automatism, letting intuition and the subconscious guide the initial brushstrokes. As the piece evolves, deliberate considerations such as composition, color palette, or overall aesthetics come into play. Conversely, an artist might start with a rigid formal structure and creatively breathe life into it, a process evident in classical art. Therefore, the final piece of art emerges from this dynamic interaction of fast and slow thinking. The initial conception undergoes impartial judgment and precise refinements, thus perfecting the technical aspects and rectifying any execution flaws. The cycle continues until the artwork fully aligns with the artist's vision. Great artists throughout art history demonstrate this dichotomy between creativity and technical skill on one hand and firm determination to manage a project from beginning to end on the other.

In his acclaimed *Story of Art* [12], art historian Ernst Gombrich proposed the idea of art as an evolving process. He noted that artists often see progress in realizing their creative vision across their works, not just within a single piece. This evolution isn't just a series of isolated events but a cumulative journey, where each artwork contributes to the artist's mastery.

In the digital realm, Generative Adversarial Networks (GANs) can be seen as a manifestation of this evolutionary process. Introduced in 2014 [13], GANs have sparked rapid technological advancements. Comprising two neural networks—a generator and a discriminator—-GANs engage in a 'creative dialogue.' This dialogue mirrors the balance between intuition and critical judgment in human artistry. The generator, bootstrapped by random variables, produces an initial data sample, much like an artist's first sketch. The discriminator then evaluates this sample against real data, acting as the 'critical eye.' This feedback loop continues, with each iteration aiming for perfection, though often settling for significant improvement.

Let's use an artistic metaphor to further illustrate the principles of GANs. Imagine an apprentice learning from a master artist. The master presents various paintings, explaining each technique. Over time, the apprentice's skills are honed, producing works of art that echo the master's style, similar to the supervised learning enacted by the generator. Imagine also a self-taught art connoisseur. Without guidance other than their own growing experience, they study works of art and nature, drawing their own conclusions. This mirrors the unsupervised learning enacted by the discriminator, in which algorithms discern patterns without explicit instructions.

The mutual evolution of the generator and discriminator is guided by MinMax—the same game-theoretic concept applied in constructing chess engines like Deep Blue and Stockfish. In the context of GANs applied to the production of visual content, MinMax evaluates the quality of generated images based on criteria relevant to the domain of visual arts, such as fidelity to training set data or the quality of textures and colors. This iterative feedback cycle refines the performance of both networks, creating a dynamic analogous to the strategies employed in chess or other games. Thus, the 'slow thinking' in the interplay between the generator and discriminator—both 'fast thinkers'—is, in reality, the work of MinMax. In this context, too, MinMax emerges as a 'slow thinker' because it compels the generator to pause in its creative ebb and compare options in generating new images that are most likely to fool the discriminator—just as in chess, it helps the maximizing player choose the best move against the minimizing one. This iterative refinement cycle, driven by MinMax, is depicted in Fig. 2, where the word 'fake' has no negative or pejorative resonance, being the term commonly used within the generative AI community to refer to artificially synthesized data and content.

The decision to conclude training in GANs is often pragmatic, based on factors such as reaching a predetermined number of epochs, as complete passes through the training data are called, or achieving a specific quality threshold, or stabilizing

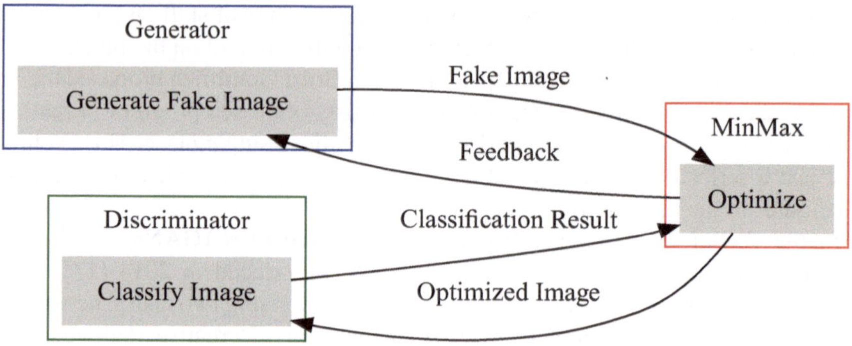

Fig. 2 MinMax-driven GAN cycle

the performance of both the generator and discriminator networks. Once training is complete, the GAN transitions to the production phase, applying its learned capabilities to generate new works.

Halting creation in this phase is somewhat analogous to an artist's intuitive decision to declare a work 'finished.' For GANs, this decision might be based on whether the generated content meets certain mathematical or statistical criteria. For artists, it could be a subjective assessment of whether the work achieves the desired emotional impact or aesthetic quality. In both cases, these criteria signal that the creative process has reached a satisfactory endpoint.

However, a key difference lies in the separation of phases in GANs compared to the lifelong learning and evolution seen in human artists—the concept eloquently described by Gombrich. In GANs, training and creation are distinct, non-overlapping phases. In contrast, human artists continually evolve, learning with each new creation and applying insights from previous works to future endeavors.

Enabling User Interaction

Now, it's time to ask how GANs can produce user-responsive art through text. Prompts and the users who provide them, the prompters, are key elements of this and subsequent chapters. How can GANs interact with them?

Indeed, with a basic GAN, a user can only ask for images without knowing or choosing what they will look like. The generator creates images that recall the training data, but the user cannot control their content. As depicted in Fig. 3, it's like receiving snacks from a vending machine that dispenses them randomly: you don't know what will come out: popcorn, chips, or whatever.

To enable the user to act as a prompter, thus influencing the image's content, GANs had to be upgraded to an enhanced form called Conditional GANs, or cGANs, which use text input from the prompter to condition the generation process,

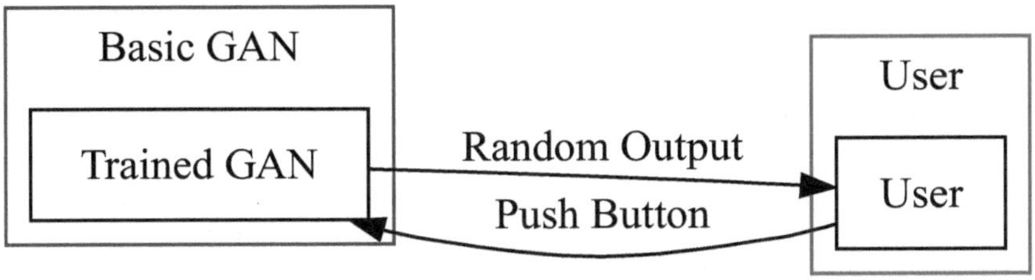

Fig. 3 Interaction with basic GAN

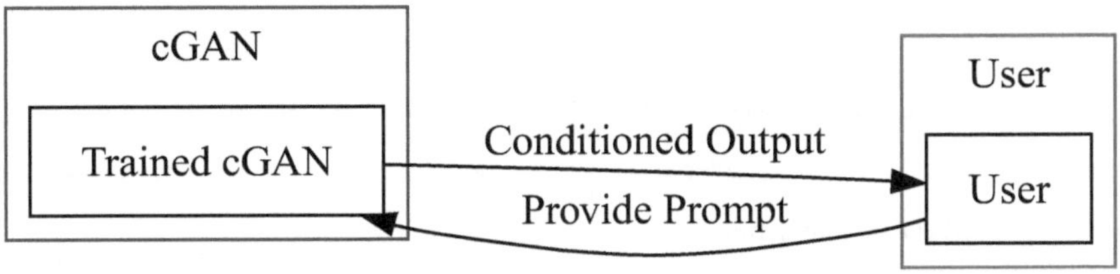

Fig. 4 Interaction with cGAN

as described on a research paper of the same year in which the seminal GAN article was published [14]. How does it work? In basic GANs, the generator starts with a random image originating from a noise vector, i.e., a matrix of random numbers that generates the first artificial image of the generator network. The noise vector is like a seed with a plant's genes, but it does not say what kind of plant it will be, limiting itself to enriching the variety of images that can be generated. But cGANs do more than that. Before interacting with the generator, their noise vector is mixed with textual information provided through the user prompt, e.g., an image category or description. As represented in Fig. 4, this enables the generator to produce high-quality images influenced by the prompter's specific instructions.

Therefore, cGANs provide a way of creating artistic content by taking natural language prompts as input. In doing so, they introduce an additional component beyond the generator, discriminator, and MinMax: the embedder. This is often a specialized neural network that bridges the gap between the prompter and the generator by converting text prompts into numerical data the generator can process. Compared to a basic GAN, a trained cGAN operates with an added layer of specificity due to the conditioning data. Once the embedder numerically translates the prompt, the generator doesn't merely start with random noise. It combines this noise with the embedded prompt, giving the generator a guiding direction based on the user's prompt. This dual objective provides the cGAN's generation process with the targeted control absent in basic GANs.

While a basic GAN might produce a random image of a cat, a cGAN, when prompted with 'a blue cat with green eyes', strives to generate an image matching that description. This capacity to condition the output based on external input distinguishes cGANs, enabling an interactive and customized generative experience.

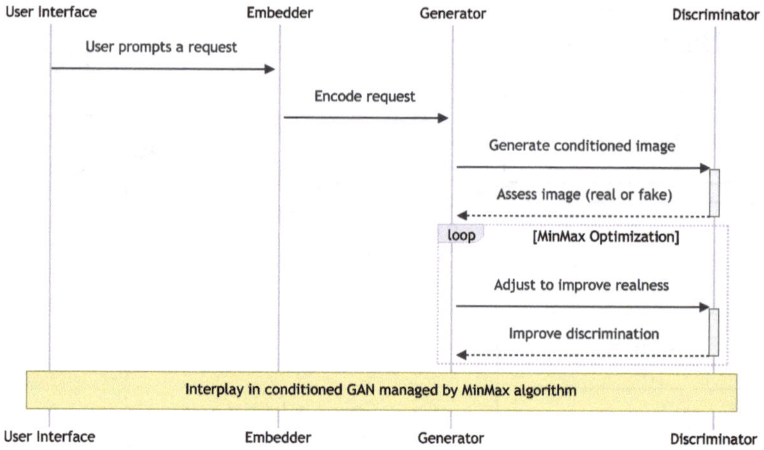

Fig. 5 Expanded cGAN interaction

Essentially, a cGAN comprises four main components: the embedder, the generator, the discriminator, and the MinMax game mechanism. The embedder facilitates interaction with the outside world by processing user requests, effectively bridging the gap between human input and the AI system. The generator then creates images or other outputs based on these suggestions, while the discriminator evaluates them against real-world data to ensure authenticity and relevance. The MinMax game mechanism is a competitive process in which the generator strives to produce increasingly convincing outputs, and the discriminator aims to accurately distinguish between real and generated data. This dynamic interaction, particularly the role of the embedder in incorporating user suggestions, positions cGANs as quintessential centaur systems, merging human creativity with the computational power of artificial intelligence. This interplay is illustrated in detail in Fig. 5, which expands upon the interaction shown in Fig. 4, delineating all its components.

The Role of Non-determinism in AI-Based Art Generation

We've observed that both human creativity and GANs incorporate a blend of fast and slow thinking. However, the two diverge significantly when concluding a creative piece. For humans, the decision to finish is subjective, often based on a 'gut feeling' or artistic intuition. In contrast, GANs follow predetermined criteria set during their design phase.

Conditioned GANs (cGANs) introduce an added layer of complexity by enabling human users to condition the input, thereby influencing the output. Users can adjust the input prompt to guide the AI towards generating different or improved results.

This adaptability highlights the role of non-determinism in centauric systems, where human intuition and machine intelligence converge.

In computational terms, a deterministic system consistently produces the same output for a given input. On the other hand, non-deterministic systems introduce variability, allowing the same input to yield different outputs. This variability is especially pronounced in generative AI platforms like GANs, which, due to random initialization and the stochastic nature of their training, tend to produce varied outputs even when repeatedly presented with the same input. Such non-determinism is a powerful tool in artistic creation, offering a broad canvas of creative possibilities and interpretations. However, it's essential to strike a balance. While variability can inspire and introduce unexpected avenues of creativity, too much unpredictability can pose challenges for artists seeking specific outcomes. Finding the right equilibrium between control and spontaneity becomes crucial in artistic collaboration with AI. Much of the current research in generative platforms is geared towards achieving this balance. As technology evolves, we can anticipate future releases of generative platforms—not just GAN-based but across the spectrum—to offer artists an even more refined blend of control and creative freedom.

Moving Toward Centauric Art

We have thus reached a significant turning point in our journey. The rise of artificial abilities in strategic games like chess and their artistic counterparts is undeniable. Building on the insights from the previous chapter, we have outlined the technological premises through which these skills have evolved to a point where human involvement is virtually redundant in chess and other strategic games of similar complexity. Hence, we can move forward in our quest to answer the critical question we initially posed: Does the human element still hold relevance in artistic centaurs? If so, what role does it play in a creative process shared with artificial entities?

To address these issues, we've drawn parallels between artistic creation and strategy games, positioning them both as a dynamic interchange of fast and slow thinking. This interaction is exemplified in GANs, where MinMax allows for a direct link to strategy games such as chess. As we will explore in the next chapter, further methodologies have been developed to create favorable conditions for integrating fast and slow thinking in the artificial production of works of art, such as approaches based on cooperation rather than confrontation between game opponents.

But alongside the technological continuity between game engines and artistic production platforms, there's also a fundamental discontinuity related to the context of use, which influences the validity of the centaur metaphor. Strategy games operate within closed environments, while art, by its nature, requires an open setting that involves interaction with the outside world; the conditioning role of prompters in cGANs gives us a first glimpse of how this aspect can make all the difference.

So, let's delve deeper into the nature of artistic centaurs and their role in our world, which is increasingly destined for the coexistence of natural and artificial intelligence.

References

1. John von Neumann and Oskar Morgenstern. *Theory of Games and Economic Behavior*. Princeton University Press, 1944.
2. Jonathan Schaeffer et al. "Checkers is solved". In: *Science* 317.5844 (2007), pp. 1518–1522. URL: https://citeseerx.ist.psu.edu/viewdoc/summary?doi$=$10.1.1.227.6112.
3. Claude E. Shannon. "Programming a Computer for Playing Chess". In: *Philosophical Magazine* 41.314 (1950).
4. Hans Berliner. *The System: A World Champion's Approach to Chess*. Gambit, 1999.
5. Ray Kurzweil. *The Age of Spiritual Machines: When Computers Exceed Human Intelligence*. Penguin, 2000. URL: https://books.google.it/books/about/The_Age_of_Spiritual_Machines.html?id$=$lbl4MN3iUHsC&redir_esc$=$y.
6. David Silver et al. "Mastering chess and shogi by self-play with a general reinforcement learning algorithm". In: *Science* 362.6419 (2018), pp. 1140–1144. URL: https://oa.mg/work/10.1126/science.aar6404.
7. Julien Perolat et al. "Mastering the Game of Stratego with Model-Free Multiagent Reinforcement Learning". In: *Science* 374.6575 (2022), eadd4679.
8. Daniel Kahneman. *Thinking, fast and slow*. Farrar, Straus and Giroux, 2011.
9. Grady Booch et al. "Thinking Fast and Slow in AI". In: *Proceedings of the AAAI Conference on Artificial Intelligence*. Vol. 35. 17. 2021, pp. 15042–15046.
10. Marianna Bergamaschi Ganapini et al. "Thinking Fast and Slow in AI: The Role of Metacognition". In: *Machine Learning, Optimization, and Data Science - 8th International Workshop, LOD 2022, Certosa di Pontignano, Italy, September 19–22, 2022, Revised Selected Papers, Part II*. Ed. by Giuseppe Nicosia et al. Vol. 13811. Lecture Notes in Computer Science. Springer, 2022, pp. 502–509. DOI: https://doi.org/10.1007/978-3-031-25891-6%5C_38.
11. A. M. Turing. "Computing Machinery and Intelligence". In: *Mind* 59.236 (1950), pp. 433–460.
12. E. H. Gombrich. *The Story of Art*. Phaidon Press, 1995.
13. Ian J Goodfellow et al. "Generative adversarial nets". In: *Advances in neural information processing systems*. 2014, pp. 2672–2680.
14. Mehdi Mirza and Simon Osindero. "Conditional Generative Adversarial Nets". In: *CoRR* abs/1411.1784 (2014). arXiv: 1411.1784. URL: http://arxiv.org/abs/1411.1784.

The Art of Turning Prompts into Art

The best way to test theoretical hypotheses is by putting them into practice. This chapter delves into the practice of centauric art by applying DALL-E, a state-of-the-art AI platform by the company OpenAI, renowned for generating high-quality artistic content from textual prompts. OpenAI, a frontrunner in the generative AI domain, is also the creator of the widely debated yet immensely popular ChatGPT chatbot. The name 'DALL-E' cleverly pays homage to the surrealist artist Salvador Dalí and Pixar's beloved robot, WALL-E. While DALL-E isn't the sole image-generating tool from text, its capabilities have garnered significant acclaim, making it an ideal candidate to explore the creative horizons of generative platforms.

Before diving into the hands-on exploration of artistic centaurism, we must round off our understanding of generative AI architectures for visual content creation. Unlike the Generative Adversarial Networks (GANs) discussed in the previous chapter, DALL-E operates on a cooperative paradigm. While both employ dual neural networks, DALL-E's networks function collaboratively, unlike the adversarial dynamic in GANs. However, just like GANs, they integrate the fast thinking propelled by neural networks with the slow thinking that characterizes pondered choices.

DALL-E's Diffusion Model

DALL-E's prowess lies in its ability to produce images spanning diverse artistic styles. Like Conditional GANs, it employs an 'embedder'—an algorithm that translates textual prompts into a numerically processable format, aligning with the centaur model's dual components: external information acquisition and structuring and internal processing. On the other hand, different from GANs, DALL-E uses

R. Pareschi, *Centaur Art*, https://doi.org/10.1007/978-3-031-69063-1_4

specialized neural networks designed for natural language and image processing. These networks work together to create images that match the text.[1]

Thus, DALL-E's functionality hinges on the well-balanced cooperation of two components, one of which is CLIP (Contrastive Language-Image Pre-training). CLIP bridges textual and visual domains, significantly departing from traditional image processing methods. Historically, image processing models were rooted in the classification paradigm, a methodological approach with ancient origins tracing back to Aristotle circa 300 BC. This categorization-based reasoning has proven effective in various decision-making scenarios, operating on the principle that the world can be compartmentalized into distinct categories. In the realm of image processing, this allows for differentiation between, say, images of "dogs" and "cats." However, these models hit a ceiling when applied to intricate visuals like paintings. They can categorize individual elements within the artwork but falter when interpreting the holistic composition.

Consider a painting portraying two women enjoying tea—one with a poodle by her side and the other with a Siamese cat in her lap. How does one pigeonhole such a multifaceted scene into a singular category?

CLIP emerges as a solution to these categorical constraints by harnessing the untapped potential of captions. Historically, more structured concepts like categories overshadowed captions, which philosophers, logicians, and computer scientists dismissed. They were relegated to the sidelines, perceived as merely supplementary to visual content. However, captions possess a malleability and expansiveness, morphing into micro-narratives that encapsulate the nuances and essence of an image. CLIP's groundbreaking innovation lies in its capacity to correlate images with their corresponding captions. It can discern subtleties, differentiating between "Siamese cat seated on a woman's lap" and "Siamese cat in pursuit of a mouse." Impressively, CLIP can even navigate rhetorical devices like metaphors and metonymies, transcending the conventional descriptive confines of captions. This prowess is underpinned by an algebraic space, where dimensions symbolize visual and linguistic attributes. This space empowers CLIP to gauge the congruence between textual descriptions and their visual counterparts.

While captions, presented as textual prompts, play a pivotal role, they represent only half of the creative process. The generation of novel images is equally crucial. This task falls to a specialized neural network called the 'Diffuser.' The Diffuser introduces a controlled element of chaos into the existing image framework, crafting new content aligning with the caption's intent. In DALL-E's context, this entails infusing noise into images from CLIP's training data that resonate with the input text. This is done meticulously, ensuring the core technical and stylistic attributes remain intact. The Diffuser then begins crafting an image that mirrors the essence

[1] A full technical description of the system's functioning underlying DALL-E is provided in the research article [1].

of the input text while retaining the technical and stylistic nuances of the altered images.[2]

CLIP, acting as the "encoder," transmutes the input text into a representation within its unique associative realm, bridging captions and images. The diffuser, donning the "decoder" role, leverages this representation to sculpt an image that hones in on the envisioned outcome. Their synergy is rooted in a cooperative dynamic, fine-tuning their parameters to diminish the "reconstruction loss"—a metric quantifying the disparity between the anticipated images and the actual output.

Adam, the Slow Thinker

In the realm of GANs, the learning dynamics of the two networks—comprising the generator and the discriminator—are orchestrated by the MinMax algorithm. Both networks function as "fast thinkers," leveraging ingrained patterns and rules for decision-making. The MinMax algorithm, on the other hand, operates as a "slow thinker," optimizing competitive gaming processes, which aligns with the adversarial nature of GANs. When it comes to image generation via diffusion models, the Adam algorithm assumes a similar "slow thinker" role. It ensures that the image reconstruction activities of the diffuser align closely with CLIP's expectations concerning the prompt's directives.

To grasp the nuances of Adam's operation within this framework, it's beneficial to contextualize it within the broader domain of local search algorithms. Local search techniques commence with an initial solution and iteratively refine it by making incremental adjustments, aiming for enhancement. A rudimentary illustration of local search in action can be visualized through the lens of a tourist's journey. Imagine a traveler exploring Europe by car, intent on charting the shortest route through Paris, Rome, and Berlin. Initially, the tourist selects the sequence Paris-Rome-Berlin, amounting to a distance of 2926 km. However, by swapping the intermediate destinations—from Rome to Berlin—the journey is shortened to 2564 km, as depicted in Fig. 1. It's worth noting that this isn't the sole optimization available; interchanging Rome and Paris results in an identical distance via the

[2] Diffusion models draw inspiration from physics by utilizing the diffusion concept to model the information flow between data and a lower-dimensional hidden space. Additionally, they employ the idea of reversibility, allowing bidirectional mappings between data and this hidden space. Another physics-inspired model is the Generative Poisson Flow Model (PFGM) proposed by MIT researchers [2]. Unlike diffusion models, PFGM is inspired by electric force fields, treating data points as charged particles. Instead of adding noise, PFGM follows electric force lines to transform data distributions. For instance, imagine charged balloons on a flat surface spreading evenly, representing a uniform distribution. If the surface is bent into a dome, the balloons cluster at the top, akin to the data distribution PFGM maps onto. The emergence of more physics-inspired neural network models is anticipated, promising innovative data generation methods.

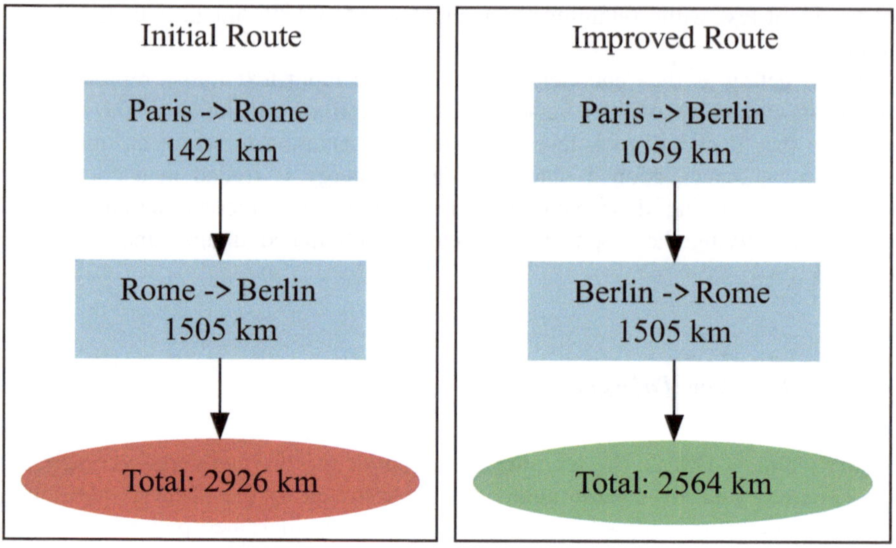

Fig. 1 Local search improvement in a route-finding problem

Rome-Paris-Berlin route. The methodology's intricacy—and consequently, allure—escalates with an increasing number of cities, as exemplified by the Traveling Salesman Problem (TSP), a classic optimization challenge in operations research and computer science. It revolves around a hypothetical salesman who must visit a set of cities exactly once and return to the starting city, all while minimizing the total distance or cost of the journey. The primary challenge lies in determining the most efficient route among the cities. As cities increase, possible routes grow factorially, making the problem computationally intensive. Despite its seemingly simple premise, the TSP is an NP-hard problem, meaning no polynomial-time solution is known for it, and it serves as a benchmark for various optimization algorithms.

Hence, imagine planning an optimized journey through a series of cities, much like the TSP. This physical traversal serves as a compelling metaphor for the role of the Adam optimization algorithm in the digital realm of Deep Learning, specifically in coordinating the efforts of CLIP and the Diffuser for visual content generation.

In the context of our European road trip analogy, each city represents a potential solution or configuration in the vast landscape of possible images. Just as a traveler seeks the shortest route through these cities, Adam aims to navigate the intricate, multidimensional space of neural network parameters to find the most efficient path to the desired image, as specified by the input prompt.

With its ability to understand and correlate textual prompts with visual content, CLIP acts as the tour guide, providing insights and directions. It interprets the textual prompt and translates it into a target in the neural network's parameter space. Think of CLIP as the GPS that knows the destination based on the description provided.

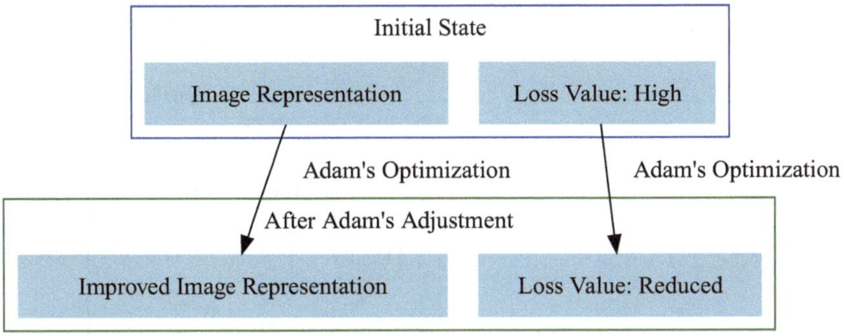

Fig. 2 Adam improvement step

However, knowing the destination is only half the battle. The journey to reach it efficiently is where Adam comes into play. Instead of physical distances between cities, Adam deals with a more abstract measure: the 'loss function.' This function quantifies the difference between the generated image and the ideal output as envisioned by the prompt. As the Diffuser decodes and reconstructs the image, Adam's role is to iteratively adjust the neural network's parameters, minimizing this loss, with incremental improvement steps as represented in Fig. 2.

Thus, Adam ensures that the journey through the neural network's parameter space is as direct and efficient as possible, guiding the system closer to the perfect rendition of the requested image. CLIP continuously provides feedback and refining the destination.

Training and Running DALL-E

While our analogy provides a conceptual understanding of Adam's role, it's crucial to note that Adam operates primarily during the training phase of the neural network, similar to how the MinMax algorithm trains a GAN. Once Adam has completed its optimization process, the system is effectively 'trained' and ready for deployment. This means a fully trained DALL-E model can generate images without further optimization when provided with a prompt. The heavy lifting, so to speak, has already been done. The roles of the various components in the two cases are depicted, respectively, in Figs. 3 and 4.

The training set for a system like DALL-E is vast and diverse. It consists of millions of images, each paired with descriptive captions. These image-caption pairs serve as the foundational knowledge for DALL-E, allowing it to understand and generate a wide array of visual content. The captions act as labels, guiding the model in correlating textual descriptions with their corresponding visual representations. Exposing DALL-E to such a diverse dataset allows it to recognize patterns, styles, objects, and abstract concepts. This extensive training enables the creation of images

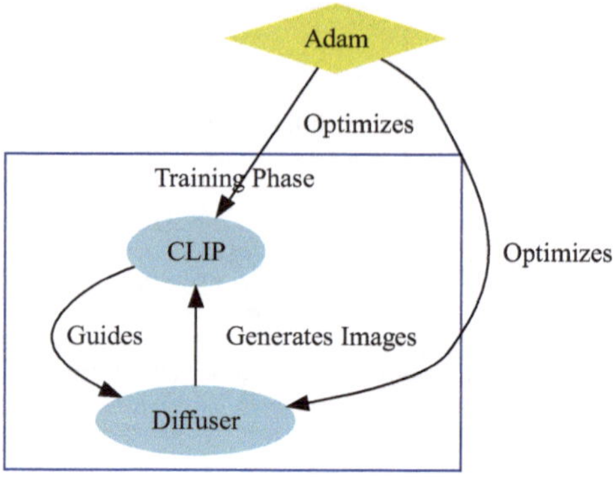

Fig. 3 Training phase of DALL-E

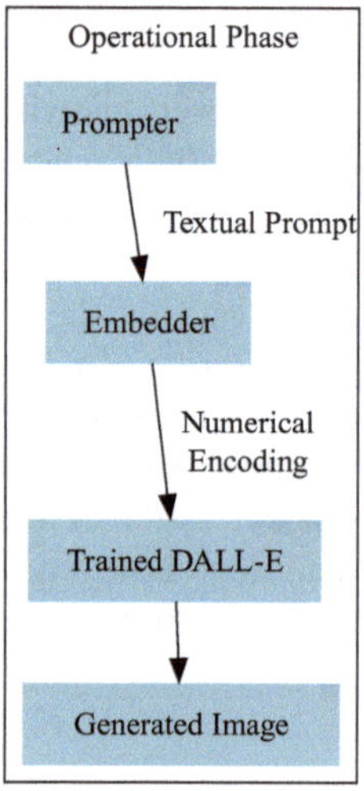

Fig. 4 Operational phase of DALL-E

from textual prompts with remarkable accuracy and creativity. Let's break down this generation process step by step:

- **Prompt Embedding:** The first step involves translating the textual prompt into a numerical format. This is done by the embedder, the system component trained to convert text into a high-dimensional vector. This vector captures the essence and semantics of the prompt in a form that the neural network can understand.
- **Vector Processing:** The generated vector, representing the textual prompt, is fed into the trained DALL-E model, thus undergoing a series of transformations as it passes through multiple neural network layers. Each layer processes the vector, refining and reshaping it based on the patterns and knowledge DALL-E learned during training.
- **Image Generation:** As the vector reaches the final layers of the network, it gets transformed into a grid of pixel values. This grid is essentially the blueprint of the image DALL-E is about to generate. The pixel values are adjusted to match the colors, shapes, and patterns that best represent the textual prompt. At this

stage, the trained Diffuser's parameters are used to generate the image, but it's not actively introducing noise as it did during training.

- **Post-processing:** The raw generated image might undergo some post-processing to enhance its quality, adjust its resolution, or fine-tune certain visual aspects. This ensures that the output is not just accurate but also aesthetically accomplished.
- **Output:** The final image, which started as a mere textual description, is then presented as the output. This image is DALL-E's interpretation of the prompt, created based on its extensive training and the patterns it has recognized.

CLIP is crucial in guiding DALL-E's image generation throughout this process. Remember, CLIP has been trained to understand the association between images and their captions. So, as DALL-E generates the image, CLIP ensures that the visual content aligns well with the semantics of the prompt. It's like having a guiding hand constantly checking and confirming, "Is this image a good representation of the given text?"

In essence, the runtime image generation results from a choreography involving the embedder, DALL-E, and CLIP, designed to transform words into visuals effectively. And, as in the case of cGANs, it is a centauric system, with the prompter—the seeing and directing head of the creature—which transfers, organizes, and represents information from the external world, and DALL-E—the body equipped with powerful motor capabilities—which interprets and executes the instructions received.

Putting the Prompter×DALL-E Combo to Work the Centauric Way

We are now all set to explore DALL-E's ability to combine with a prompter in pursuing artistic centaurism.

The process begins when the prompter provides a caption for an artwork to be generated, such as

> *A gigantic black steed, whose coat shines like polished ebony, with a glint of dark red reflections in the eyes, and with all its powerful muscles outlined and evident, standing out against a landscape of medieval castles and countryside in flames as the lurid sun sets in the summer evening.*

which the embedder translates into a numerical representation that captures the essence of the prompt and serves as a guide for the image generation process.

The trained model, which has internalized the relationships between textual descriptions and images during its training phase, then uses this numerical representation to generate an image that matches the given description, leveraging its acquired knowledge to produce an image that aligns with the prompt. The generated image is then returned to the prompter. If the prompter wishes to refine or change

Fig. 5 *A gigantic black steed, whose coat shines like polished ebony, with a glint of dark red reflections in the eyes, and with all its powerful muscles outlined and evident, standing out against a landscape of medieval castles and countryside in flames as the lurid sun sets in the summer evening*/**Metzengerstein's demonic horse**

the description, they can provide a new or revised caption, and the process begins anew.

The above quote was deemed satisfactory by its author, the centaurean artist Remo×DALL-E, a collaboration between DALL-E and Remo Pareschi. This image portrays a demonic black steed leading its master to ruin, as narrated in one of Poe's gothic tales, and was the final result of a series of attempts. It is displayed in Fig. 5 where the fully descriptive input caption, i.e., the prompt, is associated with a 'baptismal' output caption that gives an evocative name to the painting.[3]

In our previous discussions on GANs, we highlighted the inherent role of non-determinism in artificial intelligence in generating visual content. This characteristic is equally prominent in diffusion models like DALL-E. In centauric art's fusion of human and machine creativity, this non-determinism permeates the entire process. It begins with the diffuser's task of decoding and reconstructing images and extends to CLIP's role in encoding images and their corresponding captions within its associative space.

However, as we also pointed out in the case of GANs, the true essence of non-determinism in centauric art lies in the hands of the prompter, the 'upper part of the centaur.' While the encoder (CLIP) and the decoder (the Diffuser) work in tandem, guided by the Adam optimization algorithm, to produce images that closely align with the provided captions, the prompter decides the termination of the process. Suppose the generated images do not match the envisioned result. In that case, the

[3] The images featured in this book were generated using OpenAI's DALL-E model, specifically versions 2 and 3. It is important to note that DALL-E 2 includes a watermark in the form of a color palette, while DALL-E 3 does not add any watermark. To maintain the integrity of the AI-generated output, I have retained the watermark on images produced with DALL-E 2. Those generated with DALL-E 3 remain watermark-free. This approach ensures that the images are presented in their original form without any post-processing or alterations, thereby fully reflecting the generative AI systems' capabilities.

prompter holds the authority to either request variations, leading to the generation of images similar to the initial ones, or to initiate an entirely new cycle by tweaking the input text to guide new image generations.

Understanding that the degree of non-determinism in centauric art can potentially exceed that observed in conventional creative processes is crucial. This is due to the multi-layered and independent operational stages present in the centauric model. Unlike traditional art, where inspiration, elaboration, and re-elaboration are seamlessly integrated within a single human artist, centauric art presents a more modular approach. In this model, the prompter, while being the source of initial inspiration, is not the sole embodiment of the artist. Instead, the prompter represents just one operational facet, albeit a crucial one, with the final say in the creative outcome.

Before exploring DALL-E's capabilities further, we must clarify from what perspective we view this technology. There are two main ways to look at DALL-E. One of these, championed by scholars such as Gary Marcus, assesses its potential for approaching artificial general intelligence [3]. Marcus and other skeptical researchers doubt that DALL-E and other technologies, such as the OpenAI-developed ChatGPT chatbot, are progressing in this direction. The central point of their critique is that DALL-E is essentially a statistical system that generates and associates text and images. Therefore, DALL-E cannot understand and interpret its creations as a human would. But this does not invalidate the theses on centauric art.

On the contrary, it strengthens them. It fits into the perspective that DALL-E, as a specialized artificial intelligence system, does not create a new and distinct art form but expands the art rooted in the history of human creativity with new potentials and horizons. Yet this also does not deny that the contribution of DALL-E and similar systems is creative and not just technical if we see creativity as the complex result of the interaction of different agents. In this view, they can play a fundamental role in facilitating the generation of artworks, continuing the generation cycle initiated by the prompter.

The second perspective on DALL-E, of specific interest here, focuses on its execution role within the creative process of the centaur type given by the "prompt artist." As outlined above, the general functionalities of DALL-E can be tailored according to various techniques, with the final decision resting solely with the prompter. Let's delve into some of these techniques, as demonstrated by the prompt artist Remo×DALL-E, with Remo acting in the capacity of the prompter. The input Caption for Fig. 5 exemplifies an adequately articulated text that painstakingly describes both the central subject (the horse) and the ambient surroundings (the sky and medieval castles in the background). Texts of this nature are typically necessary to achieve original and engaging results.

Nevertheless, DALL-E's capabilities go beyond this, allowing artists to fine-tune the painting technique and the style. Here, one can draw from a wide range, including classical or contemporary artists (such as Michelangelo or Picasso) and specific genres (such as Gothic or Cyberpunk) to insert into the prompt "metatexts" that act as navigational tools to steer technical and stylistic choices underpinning the work. In the practice developed by Remo×DALL-E, metatexts regarding genre

Fig. 6 *A hyper-realist digital art oil painting of a part-octopus part-human star-child as in Stanley Kubrick's "2001, A Space Odyssey." Powerfully drawn in the style of Wassily Kandinsky*/**Octopus star-child**

technical and stylistic choices and those related to specific artistic references are situated at the beginning and the end of the overall text, with the descriptive part placed in the middle. Moreover, as long as it adheres to DALL-E's ethical and legal rules of use of other-party content, the text can freely draw upon cultural references from various contexts, such as novels, films, dramas, etc.

Imitative creativity, inspired by the sixteenth-century Mannerist movement we illustrated earlier, can thus be put fruitfully to work. A typical example is given in Fig. 6 and its associated input and output captions.

The concept meant to emerge figuratively is the star-child, a being sufficiently evolved to go beyond its planetary niche and explore and populate the universe, as conceived in one of the milestones of science fiction cinema, *2001: A Space Odyssey*, with the variant that humanity has disappeared from Earth; hence to carry out the feat is another intelligent species descending from the octopuses of today. These creatures are even now considered intellectually gifted. It is assumed here that, through millions of years, they will have developed cerebral capabilities and a body plan partly converging with the human ones. The introductory metatext indicates that it is a digital reproduction of the oil technique that dominated the painting of past centuries. The concluding metatext indicates the import of the style of Wassily Kandinsky, one of the pioneers of abstract art at the turn of the twentieth century, recognized for his evocative astral themes, as illustrated in chapter 2 of this book ("Art and Artificial Intelligence Between Past, Present and Future"). The term "hyper-realist" is used in the preamble to prevent excessive abstraction. Referring to Kubrick's original star-child enables converging on the desired effect.

Interestingly, the idea of a star-child octopus came to Remo×DALL-E from the centaur's DALL-E side following a previous production round. The Remo side had indeed planned a series of images depicting the evolution of octopuses from their current state to progressively increasing intelligence, eventually emerging from the waters and bringing natural general intelligence back to Earth a second time after humanity, either out of its responsibility or by natural calamity, had burnt the chance it had gotten on the matter. To portray a stage in this evolution, Remo produced the following text:

> *A hyper-realist digital art oil painting of a Cthulhu creature as the leader of a group of intelligent-looking creatures reminiscent of octopuses and using their tentacles as limbs. Metaphysically drawn in the style of Giorgio De Chirico.*

The essence of this endeavor is to creatively merge the iconic imagery of Cthulhu from H.P. Lovecraft's horror stories with the metaphysical style of Italian surrealist painter Giorgio De Chirico. Lovecraft's Cthulhu, a monstrous entity combining aspects of an octopus, dragon, and human, is reimagined through De Chirico's lens, known for his enigmatic and disharmonious figures that echo Mannerism. The goal was to transform the horror-laden Cthulhu into a benign, intelligent creature suitable for a future where such beings could create a prosperous and peaceful civilization. De Chirico's abstract, humanoid forms provided an adequate stylistic bridge for this transformation.

DALL-E interpreted these prompts with a focus on leadership qualities, as evidenced by the physiognomy of the figures in the generated images. Figures 7 and 8 showcase the most compelling results. The first image presents a powerful octopus-like creature with prominent tentacles and a large head, set in a landscape

Fig. 7 *A hyper-realist digital art oil painting of a Cthulhu creature as the leader of a group of intelligent-looking creatures reminiscent of octopuses and using their tentacles as limbs. Metaphysically drawn in the style of Giorgio De Chirico*/**A majestic land octopus**

Fig. 8 *A hyper-realist digital art oil painting of a Cthulhu creature as the leader of a group of intelligent-looking creatures reminiscent of octopuses and using their tentacles as limbs. Metaphysically drawn in the style of Giorgio De Chirico*/**An anthropomorphic octopus**

Fig. 9 *A surrealist digital art baroque 3D render of the full figures of a Siamese cat and a Bengal tiger merging into each other in a topological torus. Powerfully drawn in the style of Magritte*/**Feline ring**

hinting at an advanced civilization where this being holds a significant role. The second image, however, surpasses initial expectations by depicting a hybrid entity, part octopus and part human, surrounded by a group of followers. This unexpected result inspired a new direction in the creative process. It led to conceptualizing these images as evolutionary stages in the life of these future octopuses, culminating in a scene of cosmic exploration, as depicted in Fig. 6.

This iterative process of co-creation, which has been a common occurrence in similar experiments, exemplifies the complementary nature of the human-AI partnership in artistic creation. It demonstrates a dynamic, two-way interaction: not only does the human prompter guide the AI in generating concepts, but the AI's outputs can also inspire the prompter to develop new, unforeseen ideas. This reciprocal relationship enriches the creative process, allowing the exploration of novel artistic territories that neither humans nor AI can independently achieve.

In chapter "Art and Artificial Intelligence Between Past, Present and Future", we explored how artistic movements like Cubism, pioneered by Braque and Picasso in the early twentieth century, could inspire a broader 'geometrism' enabled by the power of generative AI. Figure 9 illustrates this idea, with DALL-E demonstrating its potential to cope with complex spatial concepts such as topological forms and incorporating Magritte's stylistic features to impart a surreal touch to the unusual feline blend depicted there.

Capturing Spatial Relationships: Work in Progress

While DALL'E's results are impressive, there remains room for improvements, which could be achievable shortly in a context where artificial intelligence is constantly evolving, driven by increasingly advanced machine learning models. These areas help us measure the platforms' progress by repeating the same task with updated underlying models, as has been done for conversational AI models like GPT [3].

Let us address this issue by focusing on the most relevant challenge for generative AIs in the visual domain: dealing with prompts that involve specific numbers and spatial relationships of entities. Difficulties encountered in this regard corroborate the view that the underlying models lack semantic understanding of what the prompt is asking for; therefore, they can only produce high-quality images by matching captions with existing images statistically, but they cannot handle requests that need an effective understanding of the scene to be created. These arguments may have a certain plausibility, but it is also true that ongoing progress in this area promises decisive improvements.

Consider, for instance, a scene from the famous adventure novel *White Fang* by Jack London [4], depicting two men and their sled dog team on a journey to deliver the coffin of a British explorer to a city in the remote North. At the same time, a pack of hungry wolves pursues them. The dogs are six in number, with the men positioned, respectively, one behind and the other in front of the sled. Attempts to reproduce the scene with DALL-E's release 2, which enabled the exciting and satisfying experiments reported above, were unsatisfactory: either the dogs were the wrong number, or they were dissociated from the sled in no particular order, or both. Similarly, achieving two human figures correctly positioned around the sled has been impossible. Each attempt resulted in, at most, a solitary man disconnected from the rest of the scene. Differentiating the wolves from the dogs and introducing the theme of their opposition was even more irksome. In the novel, the ravenous wolves see the well-fed dogs and the two men as potential food sources, leading them to besiege the group.

The considerably simplified version given by the following description

Two men wrapped up to shelter from the cold, running in the snow under the blue starry sky behind an unmanned sled pulled by a pack of 6 dogs.

produced outputs that were all completely inadequate and far from the required result, one of which is exemplified by Fig. 10.

Marked improvements were obtained with DALL-E's release 3, which aimed to address these challenges.[4] Two results are shown in Figs. 11 and 12.

The improvement is substantial in both cases, even if the yield is still imperfect. The image in Fig. 10 didn't even get the right number of sleds, as there are two instead of one, possibly missing the fact the 'two' in the prompt referred to the men rather than to the sled, which is not the case with both of the latter figures. The exact number of dogs is missed, but they are positioned and framed correctly with the sled. In Fig. 11, the two men are positioned as requested behind the sled. Yet, they appear static compared to the dynamism of the pulling dogs, and their clothing is more that of cold refugees than well-equipped explorers of the far north. These defects are overcome in Fig. 12, even if the positioning of the two men in front of

[4] https://openai.com/dall-e-3.

Fig. 10 *Two men wrapped up to shelter from the cold, running in the snow under the blue starry sky behind an unmanned sled pulled by a pack of 6 dogs/***Dogs, men, sleds arranged randomly on the snow**

Fig. 11 *Two men wrapped up to shelter from the cold, running in the snow under the blue starry sky behind an unmanned sled pulled by a pack of 6 dogs/***Two cold men behind the sled**

Fig. 12 *Two men wrapped up to shelter from the cold, running in the snow under the blue starry sky behind an unmanned sled pulled by a pack of 6 dogs/***Two explorers and their sled in the far north**

the sled diverges the request made through the prompt. The progress is, therefore, evident, and we can expect future releases to close the gap completely.

Crossing the Gate of the Centauric Era

We have delved into the vast expressive capabilities of generative platforms like DALL-E and their alignment with the centauric paradigm of hybrid creativity. The inner workings of DALL-E, grounded in diffusion models, have been elucidated. These models are the backbone of leading platforms renowned for their extensive user bases and exceptional quality, such as DALL-E itself and others like Stable Diffusion,[5] MidJourney,[6] and Firefly[7] by Adobe, a trailblazer in graphic tools ranging from Acrobat to Photoshop, which has now entered the generative AI arena.

GANs, which pioneered the generation of visual content, are still popular for projects that train on specific datasets but are less flexible in handling complex textual prompts than diffusion models that interact with caption managers such as CLIP. Yet they have the advantage of being less resource-intensive and still yield high-caliber images. There is, however, a trend of reviving GANs on generalist platforms, as shown by projects like GigaGan [6].

A common thread among these diverse engines is the fusion of "fast thinking" mechanisms, rooted in machine learning, with "slow thinking" mechanisms that emulate reasoning processes. This mirrors the interplay of rapid and deliberate thought processes inherent in conventional artistic endeavors. For the centauric artist, these platforms present a spectrum of choices reminiscent of the many techniques and movements that have punctuated human artistic history, from frescoes to oil paintings to murals. The centauric artist is empowered to select the one that resonates most with their objectives, inclinations, and visions from this rich tapestry of contemporary options and others that will inevitably surface as the field continues its relentless evolution.

As we transition to the subsequent chapters, our focus will sharpen. We aim to delve deeper into the prompt artist's vast potential, leveraging language's potency as a conduit to the visual domain. Furthermore, we will critically assess the artistic centaur's sustainability and future trajectory. Will it be a fleeting phenomenon, akin to chess centaurs, or will it carve a lasting niche, continually adapting and making indelible contributions to the art world's future?

[5] Stable Diffusion evolved from a cornerstone research contribution to Diffusion models, described in the article [5].

[6] MidJourney has not officially disclosed the technology it is based upon, though there are indications that it may be a variation of the Stable Diffusion model.

Source: https://nerdschalk.com/does-midjourney-use-stable-diffusion/.

[7] Source: https://research.adobe.com/news/adobe-research-is-helping-shape-the-future-of-generative-ai-for-creative-expression-with-firefly/.

References

1. Aditya Ramesh et al. "Hierarchical Text-Conditional Image Generation with CLIP Latents". In: *CoRR* abs/2204.06125 (2022). arXiv: 2204.06125. DOI: https://doi.org/10.48550/arXiv.2204.06125.
2. Yilun Xu et al. "Poisson Flow Generative Models". In: *NeurIPS*. 2022. URL: http://papers.nips.cc/paper%5C_files/paper/2022/hash/6ad68a54eaa8f9bf6ac698b02ec05048-Abstract-Conference.html.
3. Gary Marcus, Ernest Davis, and Scott Aaronson. "A very preliminary analysis of DALL-E 2". In: *CoRR* abs/2204.13807 (2022). arXiv: 2204.13807. DOI: https://doi.org/10.48550/arXiv.2204.13807.
4. Jack London. *White Fang*. Original date of publication: 1906. Courier Corporation, 1991.
5. Robin Rombach et al. "High-Resolution Image Synthesis with Latent Diffusion Models". In: *IEEE/CVF Conference on Computer Vision and Pattern Recognition, CVPR 2022, New Orleans, LA, USA, June 18–24, 2022*. IEEE, 2022, pp. 10674–10685. DOI: https://doi.org/10.1109/CVPR52688.2022.01042.
6. Minguk Kang et al. "Scaling up GANs for Text-to-Image Synthesis". In: *IEEE/CVF Conference on Computer Vision and Pattern Recognition, CVPR 2023, Vancouver, BC, Canada, June 17–24, 2023*. IEEE, 2023, pp. 10124–10134. DOI: https://doi.org/10.1109/CVPR52729.2023.00976.

Art as an Open System

As we delve further into centauric art, it is crucial to understand that its reach surpasses the phenomenon of the 'prompt artist.' Although this manifestation of artistic centaurism was the most immediate consequence of the emergence of generative platforms, we can consider it the tip of the iceberg. These platforms have given voice to those who lack traditional artistic skills but can contribute an original narrative touch. However, our exploration doesn't stop with this new wave of digital creators. Our goal is to show how the centauric art blends perfectly with the broad fabric of traditional art, as it has been intertwined over the millennia.

In this light, centauric art emerges as a natural progression resting upon the fundamental pillars of artistic expression established since the dawn of human civilization. Our journey will trace two interconnected paths: first, examining the intrinsic nature of art as an *open system*, organically inclined to embrace and evolve with innovations such as generative platforms; second, highlighting those pioneering artists who put in practice more advanced forms of centaurism through their work, illuminating its vast potential.

Closed Systems and Open Systems

A system is a natural or man-made collection of interrelated components coordinating into a single behavior. This definition finds applications across various disciplines, such as physics, biology, the social sciences, and computer science. Systems are typically categorized based on their interactions with the environment:

- **Closed Systems:** These are largely isolated, with minimal external interactions.
- **Open Systems:** Continuously interacting with their surroundings, they exchange energy, matter, or information.

R. Pareschi, *Centaur Art*, https://doi.org/10.1007/978-3-031-69063-1_5

It's crucial to note that these definitions are not absolutes. For instance, a sealed wine bottle might seem like a closed system in the context of wine aging, but it remains influenced by external factors.

Initially designed for strategy games, centaur models have found broader and more fruitful applications, such as government, military, education, healthcare, finance, consulting, and the focus of our discussion here, i.e., art. Strategy games function as closed systems, confining players to a pre-established environment dictated by the game's rules. Instead, artists operate within open systems, continually interacting with their environment and translating external stimuli into artistic creations. This distinction highlights why algorithms excel at strategy games, even making human involvement redundant, while the dynamic nature of art remains open to human intervention despite advanced AI platforms.

Recognizing the distinction between open and closed systems in art and strategy games underscores the pivotal role of cognitive processes.

A Cognitive Architecture for the Art System

As we pointed out, the concept of a system, whether open or closed, is very general. Each system that falls into either category has unique characteristics requiring specific in-depth analysis to be fully understood. In the case of art, its specificity derives from the artist's role in transforming external stimuli into works of art. Let's, therefore, examine its functioning through a cognitive architecture that reconstructs this dynamic of input and output enacted by the artistic mind. An immediate result of this effort is consolidating the perspective that views centauric models as durable and valid in the artistic field.

In doing this, we do not actually have to start from scratch. Indeed, an important precedent of cognitive architecture that has found wide use in a context close to art, such as design, is extendable to our case. This is the architecture introduced by Herbert Simon in his book *The Sciences of the Artificial* [1].

Herbert A. Simon was a polymath who significantly contributed to various disciplines, including economics, artificial intelligence, and design. He won a Nobel Prize in economics and is considered one of the founding fathers of artificial intelligence. *The Sciences of the Artificial* is a classic in design. We have previously encountered Simon during our discussion on chess and strategy games, where we mentioned his prediction that AI would overtake human players in this sector. Although his prediction was correct, it was too optimistic as he missed the right date by 30 years.

Simon's approach to design builds on the assumption that the artificial dimension has always been intrinsic to *Homo Sapiens*, as, from the earliest technological interventions in nature, such as the advent of agriculture and the birth of urban settlements, it has intertwined with our species. For this reason, Simon divided the sciences into two main categories: the "sciences of the natural" and the "sciences of the artificial." The former investigates natural phenomena, using

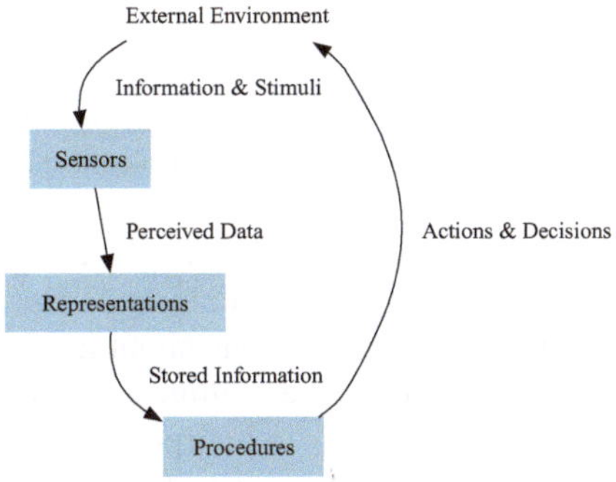

Fig. 1 Simon's cognitive architecture from *The Sciences of the Artificial*

empirical observation, experimentation, and mathematical modeling to explore physical systems, biological evolution, and ecosystem dynamics. On the other hand, the "sciences of the artificial" focuses on artificial systems, such as buildings, machines, software, and organizations. For Simon, artificial systems require a specific scientific approach, not bound by the laws of nature but rather shaped by their designers' and users' goals and intentions. This perspective has gained broad consensus and popularity and underpins our exploration of centaur art's present and potential future.

Simon's conceptualization of human cognition rests on the interface between the external environment and internal processing capabilities. The external world is a source of information and stimuli organized and interpreted by the internal mental faculties. The resulting cognitive architecture comprises the following three essential components, whose interaction is graphically illustrated in Fig. 1:

- **Sensors:** These mechanisms facilitate our interaction with the world by perceiving and receiving information. Sensors can range from primary senses such as sight, hearing, and touch to sophisticated man-made tools such as imaging devices and radars. They also extend to more abstract abilities, such as intuition or memory.
- **Representations:** These are the internal mental constructs used to classify and store information gathered from the environment. Representations can take various forms, such as symbols, images, and concepts, up to more complex systems, such as models or theories.
- **Procedures:** Procedures operate internally by processing and interpreting the information contained in the representations. They include cognitive operations such as reasoning, problem-solving, and decision-making.

Simon's cognitive model effectively encapsulates the complex relationship between the external environment and internal cognitive mechanisms. Its versatility spans many disciplines, from engineering and design to organizational planning and decision-making. To illustrate its application, let's consider how a civil engineer would utilize their creative and operational skills according to Simon's model:

1. **Sensing:** The engineer deploys artificial sensors, such as surveying tools, aerial imagery, and ground-penetrating radar, to gather information about the project environment. Specific project requirements, such as the type and size of the structure, material specifications, and applied regulatory standards, are also captured.
2. **Representation:** The engineer represents the gathered information through project drawings, models, and diagrams. These tools aid in visualizing the project and facilitate decisions about materials, design, and construction methods.
3. **Procedures:** The engineer uses reasoning, problem-solving, and decision-making methods to interpret the information transferred into the representations, focusing on assessing the feasibility and cost of various design options to determine the best course of action.
4. **Feedback:** The engineer collects feedback to update representations and procedures as the project progresses. For example, if unanticipated problems arise during construction, new information is gathered and analyzed to overcome the roadblock.

This loop continues throughout the project, from planning to construction and final inspection, with the engineer's cognitive architecture guiding each step.

Let's now consider how the same approach could apply to a discipline like painting. The juxtaposition of engineering's procedural rigidity and art's expressive freedom may seem jarring, yet the architecture's application remains surprisingly clear:

1. **Sensing:** The painter uses visual perception and potential tools like cameras or sketchbooks to capture visual references and ideas, gathering information about the surroundings, objects, people, and emotions.
2. **Representation:** Based on the information gathered, the painter forms images, color schemes, and concepts using sketches, drawings, or color swatches to organize and refine these representations.
3. **Procedures:** The painter interprets the stored information in the mental and physical representations, developing the artwork through reasoning, problem-solving, and decision-making. They experiment with different techniques, materials, and color combinations to bring their vision to life.
4. **Feedback:** As the artwork evolves, the painter gathers feedback from the external world, viewers' reactions, and their internal reflections. They use this feedback to update the current representations and refine procedures to achieve the desired outcome.

The painter's cognitive architecture guides the initial idea to the final details, using available information and processing abilities to make decisions and solve problems.

Simon's cognitive architecture offers a comprehensive framework for understanding human problem-solving across various domains, including art. However, it faces limitations when considering recent advancements in cognitive science, particularly the concept of embodiment in cognition.[1] Embodiment theory posits that cognition is not solely about symbolic representations but also involves concrete sensorimotor interactions with the environment. This perspective challenges the traditional view of cognition as modular, sequential, and centralized, proposing instead a distributed, parallel, and decentralized process encompassing the entire body, brain, and world.

The concept of embodied cognition also profoundly influences our understanding of rationality. It proposes that rationality is more than just adherence to logical and formal rules; it also involves ecological and pragmatic constraints. This idea of embodied rationality suggests that rationality is not a static, universal standard but a flexible, context-dependent one shaped by an individual's physicality, environment, and goals. While this notion challenges Simon's original cognitive architecture, it resonates with his perspective of rationality as *bounded*. Simon perceived rationality as inherently limited by the vastness and complexity of the world, acknowledging that humans are incapable of achieving perfect and complete knowledge. Therefore, this more holistic view of rationality aligns with Simon's bounded rationality, offering a comprehensive account of the psychological and environmental factors that influence human thought and behavior [2]. Embracing this expanded concept of rationality allows us to connect more deeply with creativity and art, addressing the critiques of Simon's model, such as those put forward by Fred Brooks.

Fred Brooks, a prominent figure in twentieth-century industrial design and a recipient of the Turing Award (a kind of Nobel prize for computer science), critiqued Simon's logical approach for overlooking intuition and creativity in design. Brooks views designing as a "quest," where designers generate and explore various solutions, often through trial and error [3]. This perspective aligns well with a centauric approach, whose body plan comprises heterogeneous components, some existing in the physical world and others in the digital realm. Paradoxically, greater flexibility can be achieved by simplifying and generalizing the definition of the processing component functionality. For this purpose, we can replace point 3 with the following formulation:

> **Procedures:** The painter interprets and manipulates the encoded data to develop the artwork. This process's specific methods and techniques are not rigidly defined, can vary widely, and can include logical reasoning and intuitive experimentation.

In this way, Simon's architecture can include different types of creative processes without losing its general validity, whose applicability to any artificial creation process is recognized even by those who, like Brooks, oppose a purely logical approach. Therefore, we can generalize it further by treating the internal processing component as abstract, omitting its specific operational details. This generalization fits multiple human processing methods, as well as hybrid situations that are partly human, partly artificial, and even entirely artificial, in perfect continuity with

[1] https://en.wikipedia.org/wiki/Embodied_cognition.

Simon's vision that foresees a close relationship between the sciences of the artificial and artificial intelligence.

In light of this more general architecture, let us examine the metaphor of the "centaur" to represent the hybrid artist, as in the case of Remo×DALL-E. In this scenario, the human component is confronted with the outside world, transforming the sensations perceived into text given as input to the artificial component, which supplies the internal processing capabilities. If this makes sense, it must be admitted that traditional art itself is intrinsically centauric, founded on a clear-cut division of labor given by a component that acquires external stimuli and maps them into representations that the other component elaborates. The only difference between traditional art and AI-based art lies in the entity used for processing, in one case human, in the other artificial. However, in both cases, this structure remains coherent and can accommodate the division of labor thus defined. Could this mapping be plausible?

Indeed, the metaphor of the centaur fits with Simon's architecture well. The top of the centaur is the sensor interface, which gathers information from the outside world, such as images or sounds, and transforms them into text prompts. The underside of the centaur is the component that internally processes received prompts. An example of this process is Remo×DALL-E, a hybrid art generation system based on human and artificial intelligence. In this system, Remo provides DALL-E with text prompts that must be transformed into images. As phrased in Simon's model, information from the sensory interface (Remo) is sent to the internal processor (DALL-E). But this model also applies to traditional art, where the internal processor is human and not artificial. Thus, we can say that all art has a centauric nature. This dualistic nature is more marked in AI-assisted art because the two components are heterogeneous in nature and origin. But their general configuration stays the same.

Centauric art, therefore, has a future full of possibilities in continuing a journey that began a few tens of thousands of years ago with the first artistic manifestations given by the prehistoric graffiti of the caves of Altamira and Lascaux. This reaffirms our initial assertion: the centaur model aligns seamlessly with art, primarily because art is an open system. Its structure is now anchored in a distinct cognitive architecture. Centauric chess, on the other hand, is a dead end in human-technology interaction. Chess players operate in a closed and regulated world, relying exclusively on their abilities.

Different Levels of Openness

However, as we have indicated, the distinction between open and closed systems must be used flexibly, considering that what makes a system of one or the other category are specific traits rather than univocal and general characteristics. On a cognitive level, relevant for the viability of centaur models, art is an open system, and strategy games are a closed system because artists interact with the outside

Fig. 2 The chess ecosystem

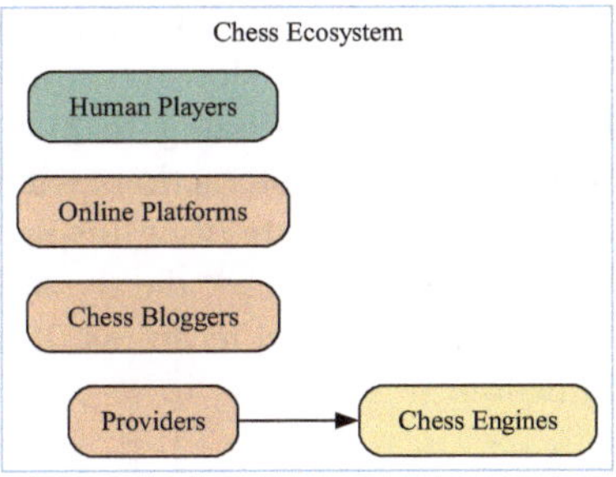

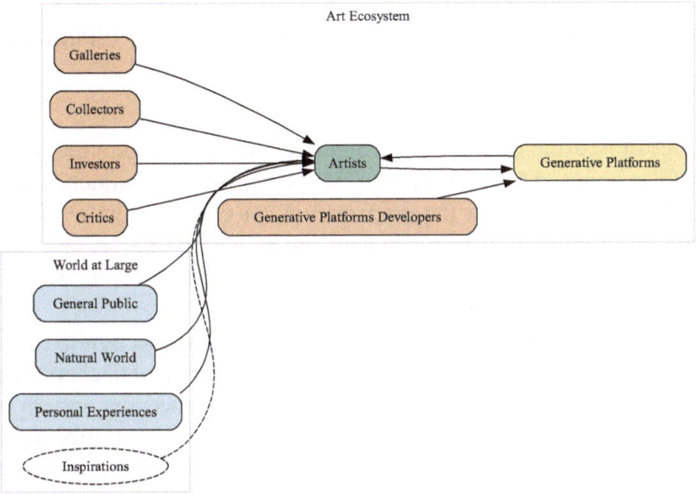

Fig. 3 The art ecosystem

world. By contrast, the players' interactions are limited to the game table. On the social level, they are both open systems, with stakeholders of various kinds entering and exiting; in both cases, the advent of artificial intelligence has increased the variety and quantity of these stakeholders. Indeed, the community of practitioners has greatly expanded due to the entry of prompt artists.

Figures 2 and 3, representing the chess and art ecosystems, illustrate these diverging scenarios. These pictures assume stakeholders within the same ecosystem engage in implicit communication. Arrows between components indicate intentional and direct interactions, fostering transformative and productive processes. The chess world remains confined to its ecosystem. It maintains a degree of openness as its stakeholders influence one another. Still, releasing and updating chess engines is the only transformative process, marking the predominance of artificial intelligence.

In contrast, the art world, having evolved over centuries through rich creative and socio-economic interactions, exhibits numerous direct and intentional relationships within its ecosystem, with artists at the core of value creation. Artificial intelligence has significantly entered it through generative platforms alongside the developers of these platforms. However, this integration remains in a centauric balance, with human artists continuing to play a crucial and guiding role. Moreover, the art world is open to interactions with the world at large beyond the boundaries of its ecosystem, as artists draw inspiration from the entirety of their surroundings for their creations. Indeed, the dynamics depicted in Fig. 2 expand Simon's cognitive architecture adapted to art, as illustrated in the previous pages, in a fully systemic direction.

The Roles of Collaboration and Language in the Creation of Art

We have thus closed the circle in our cognitive and socio-economic description of the art world as opposed to what we have adopted as the main touchstone, the chess world. We have characterized the art world as an open system allowing creative and collaborative interactions between man and machine. This partnership is hardly viable in the chess world, which remains essentially closed despite the entry of new stakeholders, such as online players.

To illustrate how the art world works, we adapted Simon's cognitive architecture, a popular and well-established model of problem-solving and decision-making. We have shown how this model can capture the cognitive processes underlying artistic creation and how the introduction of generative text-to-image platforms adapts to it in continuity with the past. We then went beyond the purely cognitive dimension, including the socio-economic stakeholders who populate the art world.

Before we delve into the various ways human art, as traditionally understood, can intertwine with generative platforms—transcending the basic paradigm of the prompt artist—it is crucial to explore two additional dimensions.

First, while the gap between perceiving external stimuli and transforming them into artistic works, as depicted in Simon's architecture, applies to both traditional and hybrid centauric art forms, it is commonplace to assume that, before the advent of generative platforms, a single entity—the individual artist—was responsible for both phases of the creative process. However, past and contemporary artistic practices offer numerous counterexamples, challenging and substantially debunking this idealization of the artist as the sole creator.

Moreover, while the prompt artist can indeed replicate, through narrative means, what a traditional artist accomplishes manually, it is also evident that narrative intervention extends beyond the simple reproduction of traditional capabilities. This is because of its enhanced expressiveness, stemming from the distinct characteristics of language, which contrasts the predominantly analog methods previously employed in artistic practice for translating external stimuli into internal processing.

Debunking the Myth of the Individual Creator

Critics who resist generative platforms often argue that genuine artists would never rely on such tools, as they ostensibly do most of the creative work. However, artists delegating technical tasks while retaining full authorship is nothing new. As previously emphasized, technical proficiency alone does not suffice to create outstanding art or achieve success; vision and inspiration are paramount. Artists endowed with these qualities can entrust the execution of their work to skilled practitioners.

Though potentially controversial, this assertion reflects historical realities observed across various artistic epochs.

The Italian Renaissance Workshop

Consider the Renaissance—a splendid era in art history spanning nearly two centuries from the early fifteenth to the late sixteenth century, culminating in the transformative principles of Mannerism before the transition to Baroque. During this prolific period, particularly in Italy, the workshop model flourished. These spaces served dual purposes: their front end, comprising entrance halls, displayed artworks to patrons and visitors, while the back end housed studios where creations came to life.

This system not only facilitated artistic production but also fostered a collaborative environment, challenging the myth of the solitary genius and prefiguring the potential synergies between human artists and generative platforms. Indeed, it offers a model that could be transferred to today's digital, AI-empowered world, as illustrated in [4].

In the context of Renaissance workshops, the collaborative ethos extended to the point where the workshop master would often sign or brand artworks produced by the team, regardless of individual contributions. This practice was prevalent in the workshops of illustrious artists such as Leonardo da Vinci, Raphael, and Michelangelo, where apprentices played a significant role in creating artworks. The apprenticeship system of the time mirrors the training mechanisms of contemporary generative platforms, as both involve learning through observation and imitation, progressively tackling more complex tasks. This historical precedent underscores the collaborative nature of artistic creation. It challenges the notion of the artist as an isolated creator, paving the way for a more inclusive understanding of artistic production that embraces the integration of human and artificial creativity.

The Factory

In the 1960s, Andy Warhol established The Factory, a collaborative hub that we have previously explored in our survey of trends preceding and anticipating centauric art. This innovative space can be regarded as a modern-day equivalent to the

Renaissance workshop, fostering a communal atmosphere where artists, musicians, writers, and other creatives came together to produce art collectively. Much like the apprenticeship system of the Renaissance era, The Factory provided young and emerging artists with invaluable opportunities to learn from their more seasoned peers. Both settings emerged as prolific centers of artistic production, with the lead artist playing a pivotal role in shaping the creative output.

In the Renaissance workshops, the master artist held a central position, directing the artistic process, while apprentices played supportive roles, aiding in realizing the master's artistic vision. The Factory, however, presented a contrasting scenario. Despite Warhol's undeniable influence, the environment was characterized by a democratic and experimental ethos, with various contributors actively participating in the creation of artworks, at times even in the absence of Warhol's direct guidance. Nonetheless, the concept of branding was accentuated, with Warhol himself transforming into a brand.

Despite these distinctions and the stark contrast in artistic trends between Renaissance Italy and twentieth-century New York City, both the Renaissance workshops and The Factory underscore the lasting significance of collaborative artistic environments. These spaces challenge the cliché of the artist as a solitary creator, showcasing the power of collective creativity.

Photography and Cinema

In exploring the synergistic relationship between human creativity and technology in art, photography and cinema stand out as pivotal mediums, marking the starting point of our discourse. Originating in the nineteenth century, these art forms truly came into their own in the early twentieth century. While intellectuals like Walter Benjamin expressed concerns about the potential erosion of art's "aura" due to these new technologies, history has painted a different picture. Today, cinema and photography are celebrated and esteemed alongside time-honored disciplines such as painting and sculpture.

The infusion of technology into art through cinema and photography has not diminished artistic expression; rather, it has enriched and diversified it. Art has become more accessible and varied, a transformation acknowledged even by Benjamin himself. This demonstrates art's remarkable capacity to evolve and flourish in tandem with technological innovation while preserving its core attributes of creativity and expressiveness. As we venture into the era of generative platforms and AI-driven art, this historical lesson underscores the potential for effective and fruitful collaboration between human creativity and artificial capabilities, ensuring that art continues to challenge, transform, and transcend existing boundaries.

This evolution also debunks the myth of the solitary artist once again. A photographer collaborates intimately with their camera; cinema is inherently collaborative. While creating a movie, a film crew engages with technologies ranging from film cameras to sound effects. The director and actors may take center stage, yet the final product results from the collaborative efforts of numerous other vital roles, including screenwriters, cinematographers, set designers, and costume designers.

Architecture

Delving further back in history, architecture stands as a testament to the longstanding tradition of separating inspiration and initial design from execution while also embodying the essence of collaborative creation. The architect, often seen as the visionary, conceives the initial design, balancing functionality with artistic expression, especially in the works of architectural geniuses. However, the realization of these designs relies on the collaborative efforts of various other professionals, including civil engineers, masons, and many skilled laborers.

This division of labor does not diminish the artistic value of architectural works but highlights the collaborative nature of creating enduring and impactful art. The architect's vision is translated into reality through numerous individuals' meticulous and skilled work, each contributing their unique expertise to the project. This collaborative process ensures that the final structure stands as a functional space and an artistic achievement.

In this light, architecture serves as a compelling example of how inspiration and execution can successfully be undertaken by separate entities, all while maintaining artistic integrity and achieving remarkable results. This historical precedent further reinforces the argument that collaborative creative environments, such as those seen in Renaissance workshops, The Factory, and modern generative platforms, are not only viable but also vital for the continued evolution and enrichment of art.

The Power of Language

Integrating text-to-image techniques by traditionally trained artists into their creative repertoire is the object of the next chapter. These artists have embraced the role of the prompt artist, blending it with their established artistic abilities. This fusion not only extends the capabilities of both approaches but also optimizes their potential. By leveraging the narrative power of text-to-image methods, artists can swiftly generate a wide array of initial concepts, selecting and refining them through their manual artistic skills.

However, the capability of text-to-image generation goes far beyond simply translating narratives into visual forms. As a tool for crystallizing images, language opens the door to entirely new image categories, transcending the limits of purely descriptive input. This unique ability lays the foundation for systematically exploring concepts on the fringes of figurative art, even among its boldest and most experimental branches. Few artists of the past have ventured into this unexplored terrain. One of these is Maurits Escher, whose figurative art is strongly oriented towards mathematics.

To fully grasp these possibilities, examining the interplay between language, art, and reality through the lens of analytical philosophy becomes pertinent. A prominent analytical philosopher, Nelson Goodman, introduced a pivotal distinction between two types of symbolic systems: digital and analogical [5]. Digital systems, exemplified by language and musical notation, are characterized by clarity and discreteness. Each element in a digital system is distinct and separate from the others, allowing for precise communication and interpretation. Words and notes, for instance, have specific meanings or values, and even a slight alteration results in a completely different entity.

On the other hand, analogical systems, represented by images and sounds, are vague and continuous. In these systems, elements blend into each other, creating a spectrum of possibilities rather than clear-cut categories. The transition between different states or values is gradual, and slight variations do not necessarily lead to a change in identity or meaning.

Some art forms, like music, combine both digital and analogical systems. Musical compositions utilize discrete notes (a digital system) to create continuous melodies and harmonies (analogical experiences). This duality enriches the art form, allowing for complex expressions and experiences.

When we generate images based on linguistic input, we navigate the intersection of digital and analogical systems. Text, a digital system, becomes a tool to create images belonging to an analogical system. This process enables the transfer of concepts inherent to the digital realm into the continuous and fluid imagery domain.

Paradoxes

Let's delve into the intriguing world of paradoxes, which may seem like linguistic anomalies or semantic misfires at first glance, resulting in statements that defy categorization as true or false. These peculiar constructs are intrinsic to language use. They originate in the complex interaction of discrete units such as words and the grammatical structures in which they are composed. Unlike linguistic expressions, visual content such as images do not have a direct equivalent to paradoxes. Yet, artists like M.C. Escher have masterfully explored and depicted them, as highlighted by Douglas Hofstadter in his bestselling work, *Gödel, Escher, Bach: An Eternal Golden Braid* [6].

Escher's art, mesmerizing depictions of impossible structures and endless loops, visually echoes the cyclical and inescapable nature of paradoxes. Works such as *Prententententoonstelling (Print Gallery)*[2] and many others serve as graphic representations of these enigmatic concepts, drawing parallels between the visual and linguistic realms.

In his book, Hofstadter relates Escher's artwork with the findings of Kurt Gödel, one of the protagonists of twentieth-century logic. Gödel's groundbreaking work introduced a paradox that challenged the foundational aspects of mathematics—a discipline often expressed through its own precise and formal language. His Incompleteness Theorems demonstrated that certain truths within the mathematical system cannot be proven within that system itself, suggesting that even mathemat-

[2] https://en.wikipedia.org/wiki/Print_Gallery_(M._C._Escher).

ical language, when pushed to its limits, encounters boundaries similar to those in natural languages. This realization that natural or mathematical language inherently contains paradoxes underscores their power and universality.

Gödel's discoveries reveal that paradoxes are not merely intellectual curiosities but potent tools that expose formal systems' limitations and underlying structures. They remind us that reality is vast and complex, often eluding complete understanding through conventional means. Paradoxes act as critical probes by showing that even a system as rigorous as mathematics can fail to contain its truths, illuminating the fundamental inconsistencies and hidden truths within our knowledge frameworks. These paradoxical insights offer windows through which we can glimpse the broader complexities and elusive nature of reality, challenging us to rethink our approaches to understanding and representing the world. Yet, in its attempt to recreate reality and offer new perspectives, art could fruitfully exploit paradoxes, using them to reveal a reality beyond the apparent. This brings us to the capability of text-to-image technologies to generate visual paradoxes by bridging a discrete medium like language with the seamless fluidity of images to explore and express reality's enigmatic and multifaceted nature.

To this end, let's undertake a demonstrative exploration using DALL-E to generate images from paradoxical sentences. Paradoxes often arise from self-reference, in that the defining expression is part of what is defined. As proof that these characteristics can easily be translated into images using generative platforms, consider the image depicted in Fig. 4, which shows a self-portrait engaged in the very act of painting itself. This image was generated through a prompt, which, in addition to being self-referential and paradoxical, refers to artistic movements and painters of the past compatible with these conceptual acrobatics.

The image that emerges is a compelling fusion of paradox and artistic expression. It captures a painter amid creation, part of whom is contained within the painting, while another part reaches out from the canvas. Notably, various segments of the painter's figure remain unpainted, highlighting the notion of the artwork—and, by

Fig. 4 *A surrealistic digital art baroque paradoxical oil painting of a painter who paints this painting. Fractally drawn in the style of Parmigianino*/**Work in progress**

extension, art itself—as an ongoing process. This visual representation crystallizes the paradox, offering a tangible insight into the complex relationship between the artist, the artwork, and the creative act.

Going further, let's test how paradoxes capture the intricate and often problematic psychological states manifesting in human behavior. Consider the concept of narcissism, a psychological condition characterized by an individual's preoccupation with self-admiration and self-aggrandizement, often at the expense of his or her larger personality. The mythological figure Narcissus, whose infatuation with his reflection caused him to transform into a flower, gives his name to this condition.

Figure 5 seeks to embody this concept, as well as push its limits further, representing an individual who not only looks at his reflection but also merges with it, entering the very mirror in which he gazes. This visual paradox, crafted through a caption that conflates two antonymic concepts, the 'self' and the 'other,' serves as a metaphor for narcissism, illustrating the self-consuming loop of self-obsession and the distortion of self-perception it entails.

In human interaction, we frequently encounter the theme of the multifaceted nature of identity—the various 'faces' or 'masks' that individuals do to navigate social contexts. Psychologically, this can be linked to disorders such as dissociative identity disorder, where a person exhibits multiple distinct personalities. Existentially, numerous philosophers and authors have been captivated by the societal 'masks' imposed upon individuals. A notable exploration of this concept is found in the work of Italian writer and playwright Luigi Pirandello. In his novel *One, No One and One Hundred Thousand* (Italian: *Uno, Nessuno e Centomila*), he portrays the individual as an essential 'nobody,' layered with countless societal masks or stereotypes.

Is it possible to visually represent this multifaceted nature of human personality—the notion of many masks? Or to depict the psycho-pathological condition of multiple personalities? Paradoxical prompts offer an interesting avenue for such representation, as demonstrated by the image in Fig. 6. This image was

Fig. 5 *A surrealistic digital art baroque synthwave 3D render of a beautiful young elf who loves and watches himself like another person. Powerfully drawn in the style of Parmigianino*/**Narcissus**

Fig. 6 *A surrealistic digital art baroque paradoxical oil painting of a man who unmasks himself to reveal his face as another mask. Fractally drawn in the style of Paul Klee*/**Unmasked**

generated using a self-referential concept of 'the mask that masks itself,' drawing inspiration from Paul Klee, a contemporary of Pirandello. Klee was known for imbuing his abstract works with an unsettling, magical quality.

Impossible Objects

Delving into the philosophical bedrock of image generation, we engage with Alexius Meinong, an Austrian philosopher whose legacy is marked by controversy [7]. To some, he is an eccentric on the periphery of philosophical discourse; to others, he is the architect of a comprehensive theory encompassing all conceivable mental representations. Meinong's foray into the realm of language holds potential significance for creating images that transcend the usual limits of the imagination, thereby enhancing art's ability to uncover hidden dimensions of reality.

At the heart of Meinong's ontology are 'impossible objects', entities that defy logical coherence, such as a square circle or liquid ice. Although these concepts are logically contradictory, they possess linguistic meaning. They are deemed conceivable by Meinong, thus existing in the realm of thought but not in tangible reality.[3] Crucially, their precise articulation in language empowers us to engage generative platforms effectively. By embedding these concepts into input prompts,

[3] Recent developments have highlighted that Meinong's ontology, once dismissed by twentieth-century language philosophers, aligns well with widely accepted logical advancements, such as modal logic—the logic of possible worlds. Specifically, the logician Franz Berto, building upon the work of another logician, Graham Priest's foundation of dialetheism (the concept that true contradictions can exist) [8], and paraconsistent logic, which tolerates contradictions, further extends modal logic to encompass 'impossible worlds.' In these realms, Meinong's impossible objects find a place, enabling their use within inferential processes [9].

Fig. 7 *A surrealistic digital art painting of King Arthur and the knights of the square round table in ancient Camelot*/**Camelot's decline**

we task the platform to resolve their inherent logical dissonances, thereby enabling the generation of visual content that is both unpredictable and enlightening.

In an intriguing blend of myth and paradox, the image depicted in Fig. 7 emerges from a prompt challenging the generative model to reconcile the legendary Arthurian fellowship with a geometrically impossible 'square round table.' The resulting image cleverly navigates the contradiction by casting a polygonal shadow beneath an otherwise circular table. The knights themselves are arranged in a disarray that belies the legendary order typically associated with Arthur's court. Some stand, others sit in disheveled postures, and one knight is notably preoccupied with his drawn sword. Amidst this scene, Arthur's presence is ambiguous, and the grandeur of the hall is compromised by the curious onlookers who peer in, their whispers and stares adding a layer of public scrutiny.

Indeed, a possible interpretation suggests a Camelot fraught with underlying tension and discord. The round table, long a symbol of unity and equality, now casts a shadow of division and irregularity, mirroring the disunity among the knights. The image, if used as a foundation for a narrative artwork, could be seen as a metaphor for the decline of Camelot, where clandestine power struggles fracture the surface harmony, and the once cohesive brotherhood of knights is now a camp of divided loyalties.

Generative Architecture

Geometry offers fertile ground for the conception of impossible objects, and their descriptions within prompts can indirectly yet fruitfully contribute to generating innovative architectural designs. This approach aligns particularly well with the creative tradition in modern architecture, which is celebrated for its expressive, often organic forms. These works are conceived as direct responses to aesthetic considerations and cultural contexts, thus imbued with symbolic meaning. Within this realm, the visual complexities, born from the semantic tensions within impossible objects, can be effectively harnessed.

For our exploratory experiments, we have selected three architects, each embodying this tradition in their respective eras. Francesco Borromini (1599–1667), active in seventeenth-century Rome, is renowned for his mastery in transforming the classical language of architecture into fluid and dynamic forms. Antoni Gaudì (1852–1926), the Catalan architect who profoundly influenced Barcelona's architectural landscape between the nineteenth and twentieth centuries, embraced an organic and naturalistic approach, merging architectural elements with forms from nature to create buildings that appear to emerge from the earth organically. Zvi Hecker (1931–2023), an innovative Polish-Israeli architect whose career spanned the late twentieth and early twenty-first centuries, is characterized by his use of geometric complexity and fragmentation, resulting in logically integrated yet disparate shapes.

We engaged these three inspirational figures through variations of the following prompt, which inherently contains a contradiction that implies a geometric impossibility:

> *A realistic digital art baroque 3d render of a tall square tower whose coils rise dizzily yet functionally to dominate the entire city, ingeniously drawn in the style of* ***[Francesco Borromini/Antoni Gaudì/Zvi Hecker].***

Despite its formal contradiction, this description serves constructively as a starting point for designing a structure that marries the stability and solidity of a square tower with the dynamic movement of ascending coils, possibly interpreted as a spiral. The result could be a simultaneously majestic and disorienting building, captivating the viewer's imagination and challenging conventional perceptions of architectural form.

Such are the expectations. Let's see how these were or were not achieved through the results. For this purpose, we have selected three of the best images generated, one for each variation, by DALL-E.

Figure 8 is associated with Francesco Borromini, the earliest of the three architects—yet it is surprisingly modern and minimalist. While keeping markedly angular, it incisively develops the spiral effect by breaking the structure into asymmetrically stacked cubic units. It is also likely to pose challenges, such as connecting and supporting the cubes, dividing and using the internal space, and coping with natural forces such as wind and earthquakes. If anything, this is a testimony to how visionary and ahead of his time Borromini was. He could create forms and spaces that challenged the conventions and expectations of his time, and this vocation for innovation has transmuted even into today's generative platforms.

Figure 9 shows a curved building with intricate balconies and a dome. It has a complex and elegant design typical of Gaudì and is likely to inherit high costs and long times to build, as were all the buildings of this architect.

It is also surprising that the image in Fig. 10 associated with Zvi Hecker, the most recent of the three architects, known for his propensity for innovation pushed to the point of recklessness, produces the most traditional building: a tall and majestic tower in which the curvature aspects are implemented only

Fig. 8 Borromini's tower

Fig. 9 Gaudì's tower

Fig. 10 Hecker's tower

ornamentally but not structurally. But, as we know, the generative platforms operate non-deterministically, and a certain unpredictability of the output is always to be considered.

Centauric Synesthesia

Finally, we explore another possibility: using writing as a bridge between the arts. Language, born to communicate, can create narratives, and narratives can generate images, as tools like cGANs and CLIP demonstrate. But why stop there? Why not use narratives to artificially explore other creative domains or even connect them? This is the idea behind Sinestes-IA, a platform based on neural network technology that transforms music into visual art. This project, born from a computer science thesis [10], cleverly combines technologies like DALL-E, a custom-engineered cGAN, and Spotify songs with lyrics to artificially emulate audio-visual synesthesia.[4]

Synesthesia is a rare gift of perception, where one sense triggers another simultaneously. Imagine seeing colors when you hear music or words. That's how some famous musicians, like Billy Joel and Duke Ellington, experienced their art. Mozart and Liszt also saw colors in musical keys. Alexander Scriabin went even further: he wanted to fuse music and colors into a single experience for his audience.

Scriabin was a visionary composer who dreamed of a total art that would unite music, colors, poetry, dance, and even scents. He composed a symphony called *Prometheus: The Poem of Fire*, which included a color organ that projected colored lights along with the music. He also planned a grandiose project, Mysterium, which would trigger a cosmic transformation through a week-long performance involving multiple sensory stimuli [12–14]. He pioneered modernism and was a multimedia art precursor who challenged the conventional boundaries of music and expression. As much a visionary as an innovator, had he lived in our times, he would have most likely embraced the centaur of the hybridization between human and artificial intelligence. And he would have been highly interested in the Sinestes-IA project.

[4] The approach to synesthesia in this project is primarily aesthetic. Nonetheless, it is underpinned by well-established neurological evidence about the functioning of the human brain. Reproducing synesthesia at an artificial level represents a step towards achieving Artificial General Intelligence, encompassing both the higher cognitive ability to produce synesthetic artworks and the more foundational neurological aspect of mimicking human brain functions. The recent book *Synesthesia* by neurology researcher Richard E. Cytowic [11] offers an accessible overview of synesthesia from a neuro-clinical perspective. The neurological basis of synesthesia is explored through theories such as the cross-activation theory, which posits that synesthesia results from the activation of adjacent brain regions processing different sensory modalities, and the disinhibited feedback theory, which suggests that synesthesia arises from reduced inhibition of feedback signals between higher and lower cortical areas. While these theories provide a framework for understanding synesthesia, they form part of a broader and evolving research landscape exploring the complexity of this phenomenon.

Sinestes-IA aims to create a unique synesthetic experience by blending sound and sight.[5] Central to this endeavor, it integrates music, imagery, and natural language processing. Spotify[6] provides the music and lyrics, forming the primary input for this project. These lyrics guide not only the emotional classification of the music but also act as prompts for DALL-E to generate corresponding images. A custom conditional Generative Adversarial Network (cGAN) then synthesizes these elements, utilizing user-selected music tracks to produce visually expressive representations that mirror the music's emotional and acoustic essence.

A dataset comprising 24,446 audio files paired with corresponding images was created for this project. The lyrics served as a key feature in this dataset, with DALL-E being employed to transform these lyrics into visual representations. The fundamental assumption was that the lyrics' text would reflect the emotions conveyed in the music. Therefore, the initial user-selected set was augmented with additional texts aligned with the emotions in the music, leveraging Spotify's sound features and user-driven clustering to categorize music tracks emotionally. This extended dataset's texts were further enriched with terms designed to guide DALL-E toward the expected image generations. The images generated by DALL-E formed the training dataset for the cGAN. This nuanced approach to understanding each track's emotional impact was critical, guiding the cGAN to produce accurate visual representations. While the cGAN primarily operated on musical prompts, the text indirectly influenced the process by identifying tracks that could be categorized according to specific emotions. The cGAN played an essential role in interpreting the continuous nature of music's emotional and acoustic features, enabling the generation of dynamic images corresponding to the music tracks. A demonstration of this technology can be viewed at the link https://drive.google.com/file/d/1KD9H1srbmRVkMoHpyHFPhc9BrzKUTewX/view, where the full version of the synesthetization of the song *Africa* by the rock band Toto is available.

In summary, Sinestes-IA represents a pioneering effort in AI-driven synesthetic experiences, demonstrating AI's ability to create complex, cross-sensory artistic expressions. While the current focus is on lyric-based tracks from Spotify, excluding purely instrumental compositions, the framework shows potential for expansion. Future developments could include instrumental music, possibly through direct emotional analysis of the music or using repositories of musical criticism for the training process. This would allow for the creation of visual counterparts to instrumental pieces, further enhancing the range of synesthetic experiences offered.

Therefore, Sinestes-IA not only pays tribute to the rich historical connection between synesthesia and music but also pushes the boundaries of technological innovation in the arts. It stands out for its sophisticated infrastructure, integrating

[5] The acronym Sinestes-IA combines synesthesia and IA, an abbreviation for Intelligenza Artificiale, i.e., Artificial Intelligence in Italian.

[6] Source: https://en.wikipedia.org/wiki/Spotify: 'Spotify is a Swedish audio streaming and media services provider founded on 23 April 2006 by Daniel Ek and Martin Lorentzon. It is one of the largest music streaming service providers, with over 574 million monthly active users, including 226 million paying subscribers, as of September 2023.'

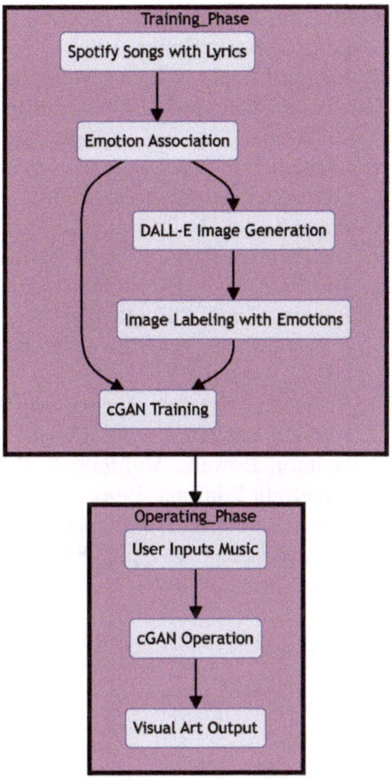

Fig. 11 The Sinestes-IA architecture

platforms like DALL-E, Spotify, and cGAN, as illustrated in Fig. 11. This comprehensive integration positions Sinestes-IA as a leading example in the field and paves the way for further exploration into prompt-based art, its interaction with various human and technological agents, and the possibilities of cognitive centaurism in artistic creation.

References

1. Herbert A Simon. *The Sciences of the Artificial*. MIT Press, 1996.
2. Shaun Gallagher, Riccardo Viale, and Vittorio Gallese, eds. *Embodied bounded rationality*. Frontiers Media SA, 2023. DOI: https://doi.org/10.3389/978-2-8325-3343-7. URL: https://www.frontiersin.org/articles/10.3389/fpsyg.2023.1235087/full.
3. Frederick P. Brooks Jr. *The Design of Design: Essays from a Computer Scientist*. Addison-Wesley Professional, 2010.
4. Nicola Noviello and Remo Pareschi. "MyBottega: An Environment for the Innovative Production and Distribution of Digital Art". In: *Image Analysis and Processing. ICIAP 2022 Workshops - ICIAP International Workshops, Lecce, Italy, May 23–27, 2022, Revised Selected Papers, Part I*. Ed. by Pier Luigi Mazzeo et al. Vol. 13373. Lecture Notes in Computer Science. Springer, 2022, pp. 162–173. DOI: https://doi.org/10.1007/978-3-031-13321-3_15.
5. Nelson Goodman. *Languages of art: an approach to a theory of symbols*. Hackett Publishing, 1976.

6. Douglas R. Hofstadter. *Gödel, Escher, Bach: An Eternal Golden Braid*. Twentieth Anniversary Edition. Basic Books, 1999.
7. Johann Marek. "Alexius Meinong". In: *The Stanford Encyclopedia of Philosophy*. Ed. by Edward N. Zalta and Uri Nodelman. Fall 2022. Metaphysics Research Lab, Stanford University, 2022.
8. Graham Priest. *Towards Non-Being: The Logic and Metaphysics of Intentionality*. New York: Oxford University Press, 2005.
9. Franz Berto. *Modal Meinongianism: Conceiving the Impossible*. Graham Priest on Dialetheism and Paraconsistency. Cham, Switzerland: Springer Verlag, 2019, pp. 3–19. DOI: https://doi.org/10.1007/978-3-030-25365-3_2.
10. Roberto Zinni. "Sinestes-IA: Una rete neurale avversaria generativa sinestetica (Sinestes-IA: A synaesthetic generative adversarial neural network)". Laurea Thesis. University of Molise, 2023.
11. Richard E. Cytowic. *Synesthesia*. MIT Press, 2018.
12. Faubion Bowers. *The New Scriabin: Enigma and Answers*. New York: St. Martin's Press, 1973.
13. Faubion Bowers. *Scriabin: A Biography of the Russian Composer, 1871–1915*. New York: Limelight Editions, 1996.
14. Simon Morrison. "Skryabin and the Impossible". In: *Journal of the American Musicological Society* 51.2 (1998), pp. 283–330.

From 'On-life' to 'On-art' and 'Beyond-Life'

In our digital era, the concept of 'on-life,' as philosopher Luciano Floridi describes [1], encapsulates our existence that oscillates seamlessly between online and offline realms. This blended 'infosphere' profoundly influences contemporary art, giving rise to 'on-art'—a paradigm where the digital and physical worlds coalesce in the creative process.

'On-art' is more than a byproduct of technological advancement; it reflects our evolving cultural and social dynamics, where the boundaries between virtual and real blur. In this realm, artists enjoy unprecedented freedom, with platforms like DALL-E evolving from mere tools to integral collaborators, merging the artist's imagination with algorithmic possibilities.

This integration signifies a broader cultural shift. Our interactions and experiences no longer fit neatly into 'online' or 'offline' categories but exist on a continuous spectrum. 'On-art' epitomizes this shift, offering a limitless canvas enriched by the synergy of human creativity and artificial intelligence. It redefines traditional art roles, heralding a new era of creativity that leverages AI while valuing human emotion and intuition.

A Centaur Taxonomy

The rise of 'on-art' is propelled by a Cambrian explosion of centauric life forms emerging from digital transformation and generative AI. To navigate this landscape, we propose a taxonomy, illustrated in Fig. 1, classifying various centaur archetypes in art creation, ranging from purely human-driven to fully automated approaches.

Central to this context are socio-economic agents of art—individuals or groups who create, manage, and own artworks. They choose creation techniques and methods, spanning from human to hybrid to artificial. This taxonomy guides these agents' artistic journey, integrating various creation methods to translate creative

R. Pareschi, *Centaur Art*, https://doi.org/10.1007/978-3-031-69063-1_6

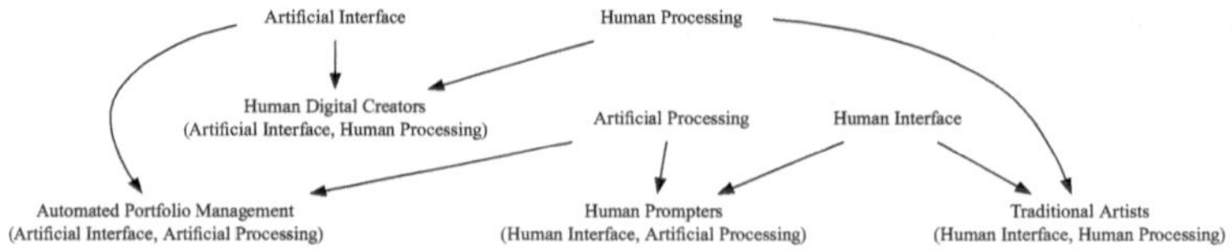

Fig. 1 Centaur taxonomy

intent into tangible art. They function within a complex socio-economic framework where art serves as both creative expression and a socio-economic resource.

Historically, artists like Michelangelo and Picasso were socio-economic agents of their work, a paradigm now evolving with generative AI. Once entirely manual, the creative process now embraces partial automation, altering the dynamics of artistic creation and the socio-economic agent's role.

After outlining this taxonomy, we explore the seamless transitions between creation modes, illustrating how contemporary artists navigate this new, dynamic landscape.

The taxonomy hinges on four fundamental types, corresponding to two options for the upper part of the centaur (human or artificial interface) and two for the lower part (human or artificial processing). From right to left, we first find traditional artists, where both interface and processing components are human. These creators excel in intuition and adaptability but face natural biological constraints.

Next, we encounter a fusion of human creativity and AI-driven generative systems, given by Human Prompters and exemplified by collaborations like Remo×DALL-E. Here, the human component provides inspiration and conceptual direction while the AI translates these into visual representations.

Moving on, Human Digital Creators retain human internal processing but employ artificial interfaces, such as sensors, to augment or replace human sensory capabilities. This approach is prevalent in civil engineering and product design, where artificial sensors gather detailed environmental data to inform human designers. While preexisting, these practices gain new relevance in the context of reworking AI-generated art, where the initial input is digital and the creative process unfolds entirely within the digital realm.

The leftmost leaf of the taxonomy corresponds to the most automated form of centauric artistry, where both interface and processing are predominantly artificial. This category, which we might term Automated Portfolio Management, requires minimal human input for initial setup. Large-scale production capabilities and efficiency characterize it. For instance, prompts could be systematically generated by a Large Language Model (LLM) like ChatGPT in response to specific user requests or through an automated variation of an initial human script. This method has significant implications for industrial design, where AI-generated prompts can streamline the design process, reducing the workload on human designers. The principle extends to other design domains, such as graphic, web, or game design, where generating numerous options is crucial.

Historically, architectural and industrial design have utilized systems like Shape Grammars since the 1970s, employing grammar-based automated generation through specialized software to develop projects [2]. However, these systems differ from our hyper-automated centaurs in a crucial aspect: they transform input into output through pre-defined, deterministic processes of duplication or variation. Conceptually, they align more with the repetitive and mechanized forms of artistic production seen in movements like de Stijl and Op Art, as discussed in the opening chapter.

In contrast, the artificial-artificial combination in our taxonomy remains distinctly centauric. While the interface automates the generation of prompts based on predefined rules, the internal processing interprets these prompts in a non-deterministic, creative manner. This characteristic is precious in the initial stages of design projects, where exploring a broad spectrum of concepts and prototypes, even those significantly divergent from each other, is crucial.

Consider, for example, an (almost) entirely artificial centaur tasked with redesigning vintage luxury cars to mirror contemporary grand touring aesthetics. This centaur could operate based on a pre-set script, such as *A hyper-realistic 3D render of a full snapshot of the external body of a* ***[MODEL]*** *restyled according to 2023 lines such that it looks like a* ***[BRAND]*** *car and bears the typical imprint of cars designed by* ***[DESIGNER]***. Here, [MODEL], [BRAND], and [DESIGNER] are variable parameters, allowing the centaur to access a database automatically to generate diverse restyling options.

For instance, the centaur's prompting part might produce a prompt like *A hyper-realistic 3D render of a full snapshot of the external body of a* ***Ford Model A Deluxe Roadster*** *restyled according to 2023 lines such that it looks like an* ***Audi*** *car and bears the typical imprint of cars designed by* ***Peter Schreyer***. Among the images generated by the centaur's processing part in response to this prompt is the one depicted in Fig. 2. Alternatively, the prompt *A hyper-realistic 3D render of a full snapshot of the external body of a* ***Ford Model A Deluxe Roadster*** *restyled according to 2023 lines such that it looks like a* ***Lamborghini*** *car and bears the*

Fig. 2 Ford Model Deluxe Roadster: an Audi/Schreyer re-styling

Fig. 3 Ford Model Deluxe Roadster: a Lamborghini/Gandini re-styling

typical imprint of cars designed by ***Marcello Gandini*** results in the image shown in Fig. 3. The Ford Model Deluxe Roadster, a luxury sports car from the late 1920s, serves as a canvas for this creative exploration. Audi and Lamborghini, luxury car brands known for their consistent stylistic evolution, provide the aesthetic benchmarks. Peter Schreyer and Marcello Gandini, renowned car designers, lend their distinctive styles to these hypothetical redesigns. Such a system can swiftly generate thousands of variations, each serving as a potential prototype for further refinement and evolution in the manufacturing process.

The integration of AI in design methodologies is transforming the creative landscape. The article [3] illustrates a computational framework that leverages prompt grammars for generating initial concepts, followed by image creation using text-to-image platforms like DALL-E. This process culminates in manually refining selected images to meet specific project requirements.

This approach aligns with emerging creative practices enabled by generative AI. For example, the study in [4] demonstrates how text-to-image generators like DALL-E, Midjourney, and Stable Diffusion can facilitate early-stage architectural design. A laboratory experiment with architecture students revealed that these tools aid ideation and creativity, especially when design constraints are thoughtfully applied. The study also highlights the challenges and potential of these tools in fostering an imaginative approach to design.

Another article, [5], explores the broader applications of generative AI in various sectors, including marketing and design. A notable example is Stitch Fix, a fashion company that uses generative AI to create clothing designs based on customer feedback. This process, involving the generation of initial sketches and subsequent human refinement, enhances efficiency and customer engagement.

Zapier, an online automation tool, provides another practical example of this AI-driven creative process. It employs DALL-E to generate logos from text inputs

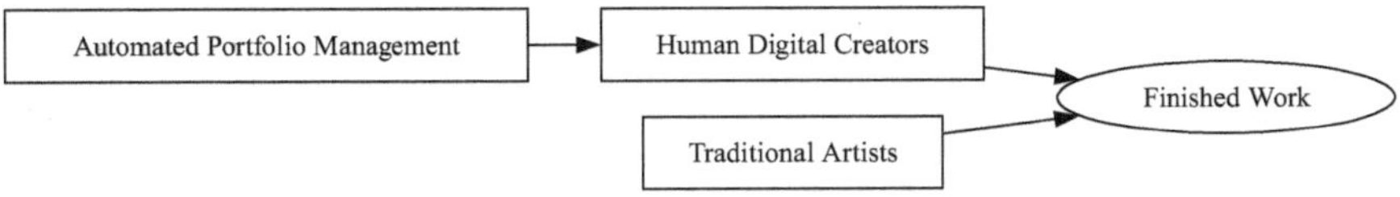

Fig. 4 Industrial design process

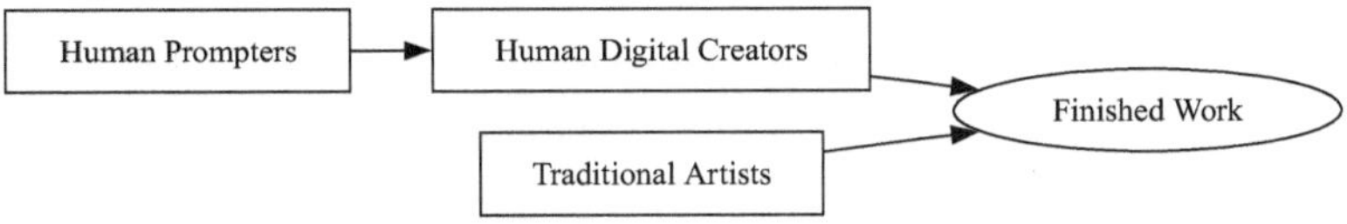

Fig. 5 Basic artwork process

stored on Airtable, an online database platform.[1] This workflow illustrates the synergy between fully automated AI (as depicted in the leftmost leaf of our centaur taxonomy) and human-AI collaboration (Human Digital Creators), as shown in Fig. 4. This combination streamlines the design process, enabling human designers to refine AI-generated images and explore various design possibilities.

Centauric Art in Practice

Now consider the creative process depicted in Fig. 5, suitable for individual artists or teams to create artwork. This process initiates with the conceptualization of artwork through prompts, employing the human-AI centaur model from the next to the last leaf on the right side of the taxonomy. Here, the human element serves as the interface, providing creative direction and inspiration. At the same time, the AI component, akin to the Remo×DALL-E collaboration, undertakes internal processing to materialize these ideas.

The outcome of this initial phase forms the basis for the subsequent stage, where the roles of human and AI are reversed. In this phase, aligned with the Human Digital Creators model, human creativity takes the forefront, allowing for manual refinement and editing of the AI-generated work.

Further evolution of the artwork can occur through purely human intervention, possibly involving physical reproduction or additional artistic techniques. This method, while contemporary in its execution, echoes the principles of Surrealism from the 1920s, where automatism played a key role in generating text and images. Unlike the Surrealists, who were constrained by the technological limits of their era, keeping writing and painting distinct, today's artists can seamlessly blend these mediums, thanks to advanced technology. This evolution of creative processes is

[1] Source: https://zapier.com/blog/create-logos-with-dall-e-and-zapier/.

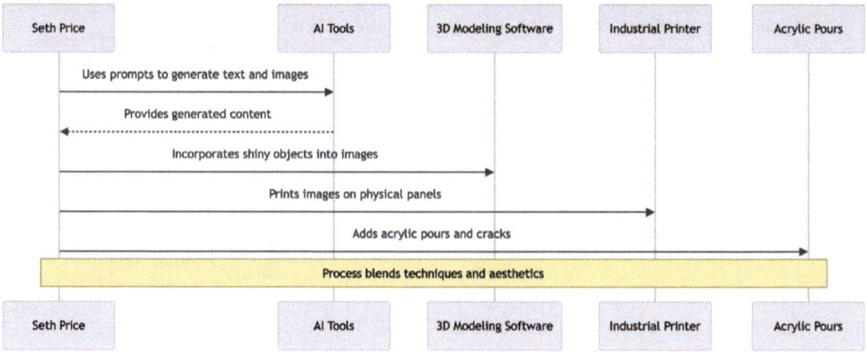

Fig. 6 Seth price's creative workflow

a testament to the ongoing synergy between artistic innovation and technological progress.

An exemplary instance of this creative process is showcased in the works of Seth Price,[2] a multidisciplinary New York City-based artist known for integrating artificial intelligence into his art practice. Since 2020, Price's works have fused abstract brushstrokes and pours with haunting faces, text fragments, and notebook-like backgrounds. This blend is further enhanced by chromed tubes and mirrors, creating a striking *trompe l'oeil* effect. To achieve these unique distortions, Price first photographs a painting and then digitally incorporates shiny objects using 3D modeling software. He then aligns them with a physical panel using an industrial printer. Five of his recent paintings incorporate AI-generated imagery, often hidden within abstract blobs and smears.[3] Price's creative process involves various phases and interactions with artificial intelligence tools, which can be reconstructed through the diagram shown in Fig. 6, providing a specific instance of the general pattern displayed in Fig. 5. Initially, he uses prompts to generate text and images with artificial intelligence programs such as ChatGPT and Midjourney. He then selects and edits these outputs to align them with his artistic vision. Next, he uses 3D modeling software to create realistic illusions of shiny objects on the images, which he prints using an industrial printer. In the final stage, Price manually adds acrylic pours and cracks, enhancing contrast and texture. This way, Price's artwork emerges from a collaborative human-AI process that blends different techniques and aesthetics.

Artists like Rachel Rossin and Martine Syms are similarly pioneering AI in art, demonstrating its potential for innovation and provocation.[4] Rachel Rossin begins her creative process by suggesting phrases to DALL-E, such as *biotech harpy in*

---

[2] Source: https://en.wikipedia.org/wiki/Seth_Price.

[3] Source: https://www.nytimes.com/2023/05/03/arts/design/ai-makes-nostalgic-images.html.

[4] Source: https://www.theguardian.com/technology/2022/jul/10/dall-e-artificial-intelligence-art.

a field at sunset or *Barbies scissoring*. She then enhances the digital output with additional detail, color, and texture. Her works, displayed in galleries and online platforms, challenge viewers to contemplate themes of identity, sexuality, and technology. Martine Syms, a multidisciplinary artist, utilizes DALL-E in her creative workflow. She inputs phrases like *a black woman dressed in blue holding a gun* into DALL-E, using the generated images as a foundation for her 3D models. These models are then animated with motion, sound, and narrative, reflecting her cultural and political perspectives. The resulting multimedia works engage audiences with powerful stories and messages, showcasing human-AI collaboration's diverse and dynamic possibilities.

As the landscape of 'on-art' evolves, Alexander Reben's role as an artist-in-residence at OpenAI, the company behind both DALL-E and ChatGPT, exemplifies a new frontier where artists not only use AI tools but also collaborate closely with their developers.[5] Reben's work, blending custom code with GPT-4 (the large language model powering ChatGPT) to generate prompts for platforms like DALL-E, challenges conventional perceptions of AI in art. His approach, aligning with OpenAI CEO Sam Altman's vision, underscores the centrality of human artists in the evolving AI-driven art paradigm.

One of the distinctive features of Reben's work is his innovative and thoughtful use of AI in art. He often begins with AI-generated concepts, which he then transforms into physical art forms. His work, featuring elements of humor and absurdity, aims to provoke thought about AI's impact on creativity and the artistic community. His residency at OpenAI provides a unique vantage point, enhancing the synergy between human creativity and AI development.

A striking example of Reben's integration of AI in his creative process is exemplified in works like *The Sentinel of Memory in the Valley of Weakness* (2023), displayed at the Crocker Workmanship Gallery.[6] This bronze sculpture was created using two AI models: one for initial sketching and DALL-E for refining the sketch into a detailed image by leveraging the latter model's capability to operate on existing images besides generating new ones through prompts. The sculpture's creation involved a sequence of centaur patterns, showcasing yet another instance of fluid integration of human and AI creativity, as illustrated in Fig. 7.

Thus, the creative process within 'on-art' exhibits many forms, even transcending the need for the intricate digital-physical interplays demonstrated in the preceding examples. Indeed, rich and innovative exploratory paths can be found even within text-based interactions alone, as made possible by prompting. Remo embarks on such a journey, leveraging the capability to transition from an image initially generated by DALL-E, as depicted in Fig. 5 and discussed in chapter "The Art of Turning Prompts into Art", to the final creation seen in Fig. 8. This latter image

[5] Source: https://www.nytimes.com/2023/12/30/technology/openai-artist-alexander-reben.html?unlocked_article_code=1.KE0.A9fp.A-S3sEwJDaxn&hpgrp=ar-abar&smid=url-share.

[6] Source: https://medium.com/@socialworldmagzine/reben-also-became-the-first-resident-artist-at-openai-e472e222fb63.

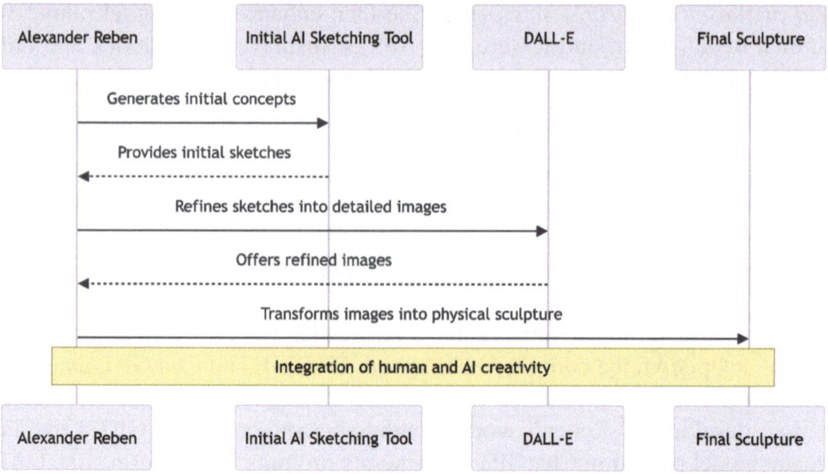

Fig. 7 Alexander Reben's creative workflow

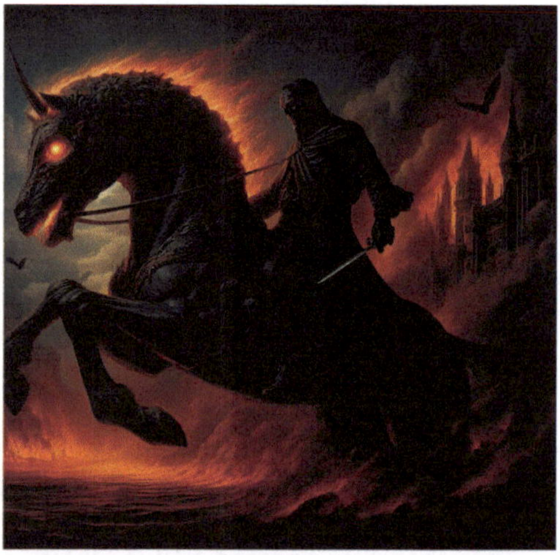

Fig. 8 *A surrealist digital art baroque 3D render of a dark and ominous scene of a man riding a demonic black horse. The horse has glowing red eyes and a fiery mane and tail. The man wears a black cloak and mask and holds a sword. Behind them, a castle is burning in the night. Powerfully drawn in the style of Arnold Bocklin*/**Metzengerstein's demonic horse, mounted**

emerges from ChatGPT's ability to craft descriptive captions for the former figure. Remo selected a particularly evocative description from these narratives: *A dark and ominous scene of a man riding a demonic horse, with the beast's glowing red eyes and fiery mane and tail stark against the backdrop of a burning castle. Shrouded in a black cloak and brandishing a sword, the rider adds to the mystery enveloping the scene.* This narrative was then refined and used as a prompt to generate the imagery in Fig. 8, drawing stylistic inspiration from Arnold Bocklin (1827–1901). Bocklin, a Swiss symbolist painter known for exploring fantasy, horror, and mythology—most notably in his series Isle of the Dead—provided a fitting stylistic reference for the prompt. His work, influential yet controversial during his lifetime, resonates

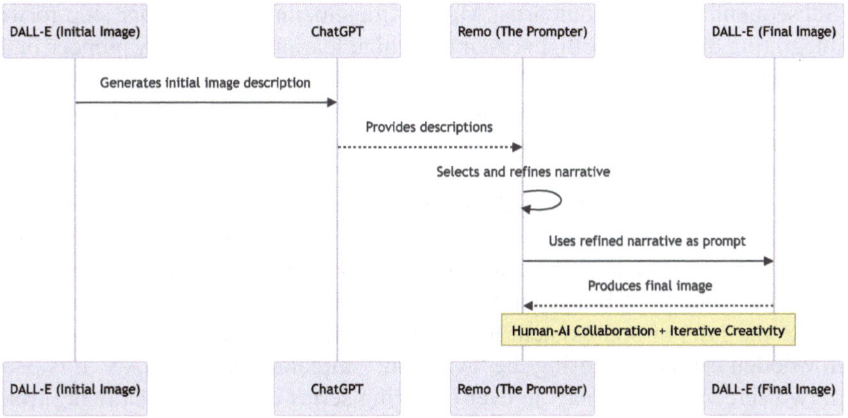

Fig. 9 Iterative prompting

through the eras, inspiring artists across generations from Giorgio de Chirico to Salvador Dali, making him an apt stylistic choice for the described scene.

The overall loop of human-AI collaboration and iterative creativity leading to creating the image in Fig. 8 is depicted in Fig. 9.

Bespoke Generation

However, artists and creators have an alternative to relying solely on powerful but generic generative platforms: developing bespoke technological solutions for generating works of art. This approach is particularly appropriate for artists with an established brand and distinct style that they wish to infuse unmistakably into their AI-generated works. Such customization allows for a more personal touch, albeit at the expense of some flexibility. This trade-off can be mitigated by integrating specialized platforms with more versatile and generalist tools, as exemplified in the Sinestes-IA project discussed in chapter "Art as an Open System".

One of the very first AI art projects, led by the Paris-based art collective Obvious, exemplifies this approach. The collective, made up of Hugo Caselles-Dupré, Pierre Fautrel, and Gauthier Vernier, used a GAN to create works such as the *Portrait of Edmond Belamy*, which sold for $ 432,500 at a Christie's auction in New York in 2018. The algorithm behind this creation was trained on a dataset of 15,000 portraits from the fourteenth to the twentieth century to focus on generating this type of painting. The portrait is named after Ian Goodfellow, the inventor of GANs, with "Bel Ami" being a joking French translation of Goodfellow's name.[7]

[7] Source: https://medium.com/@hello.obvious/ai-the-rise-of-a-new-art-movement-f6efe0a51f2e.

Subsequently, the German artist Mario Klingemann took a further step forward in integrating artificial intelligence and machine learning into art. A pioneer in this field, Klingemann's work is driven by a fascination with the creative capabilities and limitations of algorithms and the evolving role of the human artist within the AI-assisted creation process. His works have achieved international recognition and have been exhibited in places such as the Center Pompidou in Paris, Ars Electronica in Linz and ZKM in Karlsruhe. His innovative approach has earned him numerous awards, including the Lumen Prize Gold Award in 2018 and the Prix Ars Electronica Award of Distinction in 2019. One of his most notable creations, *Memories of Passersby I*, from 2019, is a generative art installation that uses artificial intelligence to create portraits of non-existent individuals.[8] This installation features a custom-built wooden cabinet enclosing the "AI brain," implemented as a GAN. It is paired with two screens that display an ever-changing series of portraits. Drawing from a vast dataset of historical portraits spanning various periods and styles, the AI brain synthesizes new faces by fusing different features into unique combinations. These portraits are temporary, never repeating themselves, thus creating a perpetual stream of imaginary passers-by. It is a work that eliminates the boundaries between painting and cinematography, presenting itself as a continuous film that narrates an infinite sequence of distinct but interconnected portraits.[9]

We previously introduced Damien Hirst in chapter "Art and Artificial Intelligence Between Past, Present and Future". As a renowned British artist and successful art entrepreneur, Hirst is celebrated for exploring diverse media and delving into beauty, religion, science, life and death themes. His innovative *Spin Paintings* series, initiated in 1992, marked a significant artistic breakthrough. Employing a mechanical process, Hirst splattered paint onto rotating canvases, creating vibrant, random patterns. This series evolved into *The Beautiful Paintings*, where Hirst seamlessly integrates generative and machine learning algorithms to both create and name artworks. Hirst illustrates the project with examples of the paintings on YouTube at the link https://www.youtube.com/watch?v=ltDVSLkKxlg.

In this project, collectors engage directly, personalizing paintings through a dashboard by selecting colors, styles, shapes, sizes, and mediums. This interactive process, guided by the collector's preferences, retains the unpredictability characteristic of Hirst's work. The whimsically machine-generated color names, such as *Himalayan Waters* and *Tangerine Pine*, add a digital layer to the creative process.

The Beautiful Paintings draw inspiration from Hirst's earlier *Spin Paintings*, introducing innovative variations. An optional 'Blur' function enhances the dynamic motion effect, reminiscent of moving paint splatters. The available shapes and sizes, square or circular, reflect Hirst's traditional formats. Machine learning-generated titles, starting with *Beautiful* and ending with *Painting*, and reflecting the chosen

[8] Source: https://www.sothebys.com/en/articles/artificial-intelligence-and-the-art-of-mario-klingemann.

[9] A video of the installation in action is available at https://vimeo.com/298000366.

style allow for further randomness and customization, as collectors can regenerate titles for the same artwork.

On the other hand, unlike other AI-focused artistic endeavors, Hirst's approach in this project diverges by not using machine learning for image generation, as seen in works by the Obvious collective and Klingemann. Instead, he employs combinatorial algorithms to ingeniously assemble elements like colors, shapes, and positions. This method produces a spectrum of unique spin paintings, each resonating with Hirst's signature style.

Hirst's project is a testament to a highly structured fusion of technology and art, combining machine learning for title generation with combinatorial algorithms for image creation. This approach preserves the essence of randomness and chance intrinsic to his art while offering collectors a degree of influence over their commissioned pieces. Hirst claims these paintings are a revolutionary new art form that blurs the lines between digital and physical creation. As with all Hirst's initiatives, there is a financial silver lining: the project, in collaboration with the software house XENI, was a resounding commercial success, generating tens of millions of dollars in weeks, underscoring the lucrative potential of merging art with cutting-edge technology.[10]

Another ambitious project aimed at transferring an individual artist's capabilities to a digital twin is currently pursued by David Salle, an American postmodern painter, printmaker, photographer, and stage designer. Salle's work interpolates various images and styles, often taken from popular culture, art history, and pornography, in a single canvas, thus challenging the conventional notions of representation and narrative and creating paintings that function as metaphors for the media-saturated culture. Unlike Hirst, who limits machine learning to generate titles and resorts to combinatorics to manipulate artistic elements, Salle relies wholly on machine learning to create his digital clone. As a mentor to many young artists, he is well prepared for the challenge given by his latest 'student:' an algorithm that starts incapable of physical artistry or conversation. This AI, developed in collaboration with technologists Danika Laszuk and Grant Davis, is being 'sent to art school,' as Salle humorously puts it. The goal is to imbue the algorithm with intuition and inspiration, enabling it to mimic Salle's distinctive style. Over months of weekly sessions, the algorithm gradually adopts more of Salle's techniques, moving quickly beyond an initial stage of bland photorealism.[11] This experiment, which marks a pivotal moment in Salle's nearly 50-year career, raises profound questions about the nature of art, authorship, and identity. As the algorithm evolves, producing paintings that echo Salle's style, it alternates between being an assistant and almost a child to the artist. Salle, contemplating the future, muses on the possibility of AI one day replacing him, underscoring the transformative potential of this technological venture in the realm of art.

[10] Source: https://fadmagazine.com/2023/04/22/damien-hirsts-the-beautiful-paintings-realise-20-million/.

[11] Source: https://www.nytimes.com/interactive/2023/09/22/arts/design/david-salle-ai.html.

Epilogue

As we conclude this book, David Salle's groundbreaking project exemplifies our journey. We embarked on a quest for answers and, indeed, found many, yet we now find ourselves contemplating new, profound questions. What truly uncharted territories might the centauric fusion of human and artificial intelligence in artistic creativity lead us to? Public opinion harbors concerns about AI surpassing human capabilities in art. However, our analyses suggest that this integration is not a cognitive leap but an extension of our inherent ability to transform external stimuli into art, now amplified by AI's technical prowess.

Yet, perhaps the most captivating question is the one that flips the most apparent concerns on their head. Could this hyper-enhanced centaurism, enabled by generative platforms, propel human creativity beyond biological constraints? Consider the concept of an artificial artist, unbound by human lifespan, embodying the creative essence of a human artist. This is the direction Salle's project hints at, potentially leading to a form of digital immortality where artists' legacies transcend their physical existence.

Currently, the privilege of tailoring artistic experiences with AI is confined to those with ample resources. However, as accessibility improves and costs decrease, this practice could become more widespread, democratizing the artistic landscape. The notion of artistic 'clones' collaborating with living artists, akin to a hypothetical partnership between Picasso and Michelangelo, blurs the lines between life and art even further. These digital amalgamations, subject to continuous digitization, could evolve into infinite artistic variations.

Thus, we stand at the dawn of a new epoch, where 'on-life' seamlessly transitions to 'on-art' and ventures into 'beyond-life.' This prospect is simultaneously exhilarating, startling, and captivating, marking a pivotal moment in the evolution of art and human creativity.

References

1. Luciano Floridi. *The Fourth Revolution: How the Infosphere is Reshaping Human Reality*. Oxford University Press, 2014.
2. George Stiny. *Pictorial and Formal Aspects of Shape and Shape Grammars*. Interdisciplinary Systems Research. Birkhäuser Basel, 1975. DOI: https://doi.org/10.1007/978-3-0348-6879-2.
3. Enrico Maria Aldorasi, Remo Pareschi, and Francesco Salzano. "Creatichain: from Creation to Market". In: *Image Analysis and Processing. ICIAP 2023 Workshops - ICIAP International Workshops, Udine, Italy, September 11–15, 2023*. Ed. by Gian Luca Foresti, Andrea Fusiello, and Edwin Hancock. Vol. 14366. Lecture Notes in Computer Science. Springer, Feb. 2024, pp. 51–62. DOI: https://doi.org/10.1007/978-3-030-79150-6_4.
4. Jonas Oppenlaender et al. "Perceptions and Realities of Text-to-Image Generation". In: *Proceedings of the 26th International Academic Mindtrek Conference, Mindtrek 2023, Tampere, Finland, October 3–6, 2023*. ACM, 2023, pp. 279–288. DOI: https://doi.org/10.1145/3616961.3616978.
5. Thomas H Davenport and Nitin Mittal. "How Generative AI Is Changing Creative Work". In: *Harvard Business Review* 101.2 (2023), pp. 78–87. URL: https://hbr.org/2022/11/how-generative-ai-is-changing-creative-work.